BUILDING A LEARNING ENVIRONMENT

Edgar Dale

A Publication of the Phi Delta Kappa Educational Foundation

Library of Congress Catalog Number: 73-185413

Printed in the United States of America

TABLE OF CONTENTS

BUILDING A LEARNING ENVIRONMENT

Foreword

This is the third monograph to be published by the Phi Delta Kappa Educational Foundation, which was established through the vision and generosity of George H. Reavis. It was his wish to contribute to a better understanding of the educative process and its relation to human welfare by providing for the wide distribution of periodic volumes, each authored by a recognized authority reporting the newest and best thinking in his specialty.

The first volume in this series was *An Educational Platform*, written by George Reavis himself and supplemented by Carter Good. The second was *The Teaching of Reading*, by George D. Spache.

We feel that all three volumes contribute significantly to the goals of the Foundation as stated by Reavis himself when he announced his bequest, four years before his death in 1970.

> The school curriculum should be reappraised, and new guidelines developed, establishing different levels of achievement for pupils of different abilities. The increase in our understanding of the psychology of learning is one of our great accomplishments of the last one hundred years. Not a great many years ago it was generally believed that much of what makes us what we are was inborn, inherent in

our nature. Now we know that almost all of it is learned.

Easy learning is based upon much first-hand experience, but the two basic learning activities are reading and discussion, and both of these are *learning from others*. Discussion is learning from others who are present; reading is learning from others who are absent. The direction of the educative process involves thorough understanding of the learning process. However, some teachers and most laymen do not yet well understand the learning process, and still believe that many acquired traits are inborn. Many traits are considered inborn because they are difficult to control. Though there are good technical treatises on the educative process for schoolmen, there is still no good popular treatise for beginning teachers, interested laymen, and parents.

We think that Edgar Dale has provided the missing treatise, and we are proud to present it as the third title in the Phi Delta Kappa Educational Foundation monograph series.

The foundation will continue to publish volumes in this series, according to Reavis' wish, as manuscripts of merit become available.

—Lowell Rose, Executive Secretary
Phi Delta Kappa

Preface

George H. Reavis was a close friend over a period of forty years and we shared a common conviction about effective communication. Dr. Reavis wanted to "provide scholars with the time and resource to complete and report studies in easy, nontechnical language for popular consumption." He was influenced as I was by reading certain volumes in the Riverside Educational Monographs which included such short volumes as Dewey's *Interest and Effort in Education* and *Moral Principles in Education*, Eliot's *The Tendency to the Concrete and Practical in Modern Education*, Cubberley's *Changing Conceptions of Education*, Kilpatrick's *The Montessori System Examined*, and Ruediger's *Vitalized Teaching*. Hence these books provided a model for the kind of books the Foundation might publish—short, clear, and interesting.

We also discussed the possible content of this book and Dr. Reavis suggested using some ideas from the short essays which I prepared over the years for *The News Letter*. I followed his suggestion and have occasionally included and amplified relevant essays from my earlier writing. I hope that this book meets the standards which Dr. Reavis envisioned when he set up the Foundation responsible for the publishing of this volume.

Edgar Dale

CHAPTER I

Shaping the Future

Things are tough here at home and all over the world. They are tough because we are at one of the great watersheds of history. We are now making, either wittingly or unwittingly, the grave decisions that determine the future of mankind. Daniel Webster, in his famous reply to Senator Hayne regarding the legality of nullification, said: "When the mariner has been sailing in thick weather, he avails himself of the first opportunity to take his latitude. Let us imitate this prudence."

This is a book on methods and materials of instruction, written when we too are in thick weather. Many predictions about the future, indeed about our very existence, are pessimistic: others are only cautiously optimistic. Some optimists believe that if we make it, we shall do so by "the skin of our teeth"—significantly the title of a 1942 play by Thornton Wilder, noting some of the close calls we have had in our history.

In critical times like these we turn to our prophets—poets, novelists, economists, historians, educators, and statesmen—to see what they have said in similar crises. In 1920, just after World War I, historian and novelist H. G. Wells said in *The Outline of History* that civilization was a race between education and catastrophe. For most of his life, Wells was an optimist about the outcome of this race. But in 1946, the year of his death, he felt that scientific advances were outpacing the applications of science to human welfare, and wrote in *Mind at the End of Its Tether*:

> The writer sees the world as a jaded world devoid of recuperative power. . . . The old men behave for the most part meanly and disgustingly, and the young are spasmodic, foolish, and all too easily misled. Man must go steeply up or down and the odds seem to be all in favor of his going down and out. . . . Ordinary man is at the end of his tether. Only a small, highly adaptable minority of the species can possibly survive. The rest will not trouble about it, finding such opiates and consolations as they have a mind for.

The following statement by distinguished educator and psychologist G. Stanley Hall might have been published yesterday:

> Old beacon lights have shifted or gone out. . . . We are all "up against" questions too big for us. . . . Hence, there is a new discontent with old leaders, standards, criteria, methods, and values, and a demand everywhere for new ones, a realization that mankind must now reorient itself and take its bearings from the eternal stars and sail no longer into the unknown future by the dead reckonings of the past.

It was written fifty years ago.

Can we say that today we know what to do to improve education, but not how to do it fast enough? Can we conclude that we know the way to make many of the needed changes but that we lack the will or the courage to make them, that we have more know-how than want-to? Certainly we know many ways to change markedly the present situation, and we know that if we stiffen our wills we can make striking improvements. But I must add what British economist Barbara Ward said in 1962 in *The Rich Nations and the Poor Nations*: "I suppose we are all aware of the fact that we live in the most catastrophic revolutionary age that men have ever faced."

George Washington once sent an emissary, Gouverneur Morris, to France to discover what kind of man the emperor was. Morris informed Washington, in effect, that "Louis XVI is a good man, as despots go, but he inherited a revolution." So it is with modern man. We have inherited a complex of revolutions, and to reach revolutionary goals in the next two or three decades revolutionary changes are clearly needed in schools and colleges, especially in materials and methods of instruction. Unfortunately, the history of the application of inventions suggests that progress is always much slower than we expect it to be.

For example, the first railroad in the world was opened for public business in England in 1825, about 150 years ago. In 1893, over seventy-five years ago, Locomotive 999 made the world's first 100-mile-per-hour run. Yet today there is no 100-mile-per-hour regular run on any railroad, and our national railroad system is in deep financial trouble.

Large-scale farming, covering thousands of acres, began in North Dakota during the 1870's. An old man from Larimore, N. Dak., once told me that when he was a boy some farms in that area were so large that you could plow straight ahead for ten miles before noon and plow back home ten miles in the afternoon. In 1910 at Chester, Mont., my father used a Big Four tractor to plow the prairie soil, harrow, and sow flax or wheat—all in one operation.

I present these illustrations about railroads and farming for two reasons. First, highly efficient large-scale farming and industrial operations are not new in the United States. And second, we have not yet solved our local, state, and national transportation problems. Revolutions take a long time to digest.

Despite our modern research on nutrition, we are not today providing an adequate diet for everyone. A Senate committee report on nutrition states: "The Citizen's Board of Inquiry into Hunger and Malnutrition reported that 10,764,000 Americans suffer from hunger and that 20 million more are inadequately fed." In 1970, 22-23 million out of about 52 million school children in 76,000 schools regularly ate lunches provided by the National School Lunch Program, which was supported by federal, state, and local groups.

There are critical tasks to be performed in this world, and a major task of educational institutions is to help perform them. The land grant colleges, established with a grant of over 11 million acres, revolutionized agriculture and agricultural education. Today we need revolutionary approaches in improving the quality of modern education. And new materials and methods of instruction can help significantly to achieve this revolution.

What do I mean by methods and materials of instruction? I use "instruction" to mean a deliberate, carefully planned effort to produce carefully described learning outcomes. To instruct, then, means to arrange a set of varied experiences to achieve planned results. Further, instruction is that part of a total educative process for which the school or college or some other institution agrees to be held accountable. They will not be held directly accountable for the many important learning outcomes achieved outside the school or college. Obviously, there will be a gray area where the responsibility for learning outcomes is shared.

To experience an event is to live through it, to participate in it, to incorporate it, and to continue to use it. To experience is to test, to try out. It means to be a concerned participant, not a half-attentive observer. Henry David Thoreau put it this way: "Students should not play life, or study it merely, while the community supports them at this expensive game, but earnestly live it from beginning to end."

The terms "methods" and "materials of instruction" are linked. We do not assume that we shall first prepare materials of instruction and then develop the methods for using such materials. The methods of instruction are directly related to the materials themselves. John Dewey says that "method means that arrangement *of* subject matter which makes it effective in use. Never is method something out-side of the material."

Effective instruction requires a technology defined in *To Improve Learning,* a 1970 report by the Commission on Instructional Technology:

> . . . instructional technology goes beyond any particular medium or device. In this sense, instructional technology is more than the sum of its parts. It is a systematic way of designing, carrying out, and evaluating the total process of learning and teaching in terms of specific objectives based on research in human learning and com-munication, and employing a combination of human and nonhuman resources to bring about more effective instruc-tion. The widespread acceptance and application of this broad definition belongs to the future. Though only a limited number of institutions have attempted to design instruction using such a systematic, comprehensive ap-proach, there is reason to believe that this approach holds the key to the contribution technology can make to the advancement of education. It became clear, in fact, as we pursued our study, that a major obstacle to instructional technology's fulfillment has been its applica-tion by bits and pieces.

I would vary this definition only slightly. Instead of "specific objectives", I would say "specified" or "stated." Excessive concern for specific objectives may mechanize learning and fail to employ the creative gifts of the learner. Oversimplification leads to routine training and distracts the learner from the subtleties and nuances possible with most learning.

I shall emphasize the difference between using meth-ods and materials of instruction to train and using them to educate. To get experience in depth rules out the use of training methods as *the* approach to instruction. Train-ing is not "suffused with suggestiveness," the philosopher Whitehead's term; its ceiling or limit is easily seen and reached. Generally, the training program is laid out for its prospective users. A trained person does not map out his own educational plan; he is dependent on someone else.

An educated person, however, maps his own education and grows from dependence to independence; he is not a slave of habit because he constantly examines his habits and makes desired changes. He asks: Why am I doing this? Is this the best way to do it?

The educated person lives the examined life. He tries to be creative and reflective. He avoids living the fragmented life, and is concerned about interrelating his experiences. He tries to become his own teacher, to become increasingly independent as a learner. He is able and willing to engage in a thoughtful sharing of ideas. He has learned how to learn, and he delights in learning. As his own teacher he can appreciate the wisdom of Horace who endeavored to "instruct with delight."

As one surveys education at almost any level in the United States he realizes that most instructional materials and methods use memorizing rather than thinking as the key instructional process. If thinking is stressed instead, the curriculum will be problem centered and question oriented, not answer oriented. The classroom climate and the methods and materials of instruction disclose whether teachers have faith that students can generate their own questions and search for answers, not blindly remember answers provided by a book or a teacher. The memory is not cultivated at the expense of the mind.

Basic themes, threads, or big ideas permeate the thinking curriculum and guide the educational experiences of the learner. The theme might be ecological; it might be related to the wise management of one's time, money, and energy. The science and art of valuing is an ever present element, and there is continuing evaluation of priorities— what comes first and what follows.

National Planning and Goal Setting

In 1960 the Commission on National Goals, appointed by President Eisenhower, made its report. Ten years later in an address to the Bond Club of New York on Jan. 7, 1970, Thomas J. Watson, chairman of the board of IBM, said that two things had surprised him at that time:

> First was the realization that this country had no very specific goals set down on paper; and second was the realization that no matter what goals we choose, there was practically no mechanism in government to methodically implement them—and there isn't now.

He noted further:

> We're trying to get the results of detailed planning without the discipline of planning. Currently, we're talking about a dreadful housing shortage which will increase during the 70's. I see little evidence that this is reflected in increased enrollment in architectural schools, in vocational schools, in new approaches to zoning and land condemnation, or in relaxation of building trades' work rules. We have to understand that if you want another 26 million housing units by 1980, a lot has to happen in 1970, and I don't think that it is. . . . It's a sad thing, a very sad thing when a nation like this one has to creep into a new decade with its tail between its legs. I don't want to do that again. I want to sail into the 1980's—and I want to see flags flying and hear bands playing.

What hope is there that the schools and colleges will sail into the eighties with flags flying and bands playing? Or will we still be explaining why we cannot do what we must do? Education can be revolutionized, but to do so we must, among other things, markedly and systematically change our methods and materials of instruction. To repeat Watson's statement: "We're trying to get the results of detailed planning without the discipline of planning."

Unfortunately, today we are still carrying over into a complex world the methods and materials of instruction of a simple society. In this simple society, the child was often a part of and a partner in the everyday events occurring in the home, workshop, or field. He physically sensed events around him, for he was in the living presence of the acts of cooking, milking, spinning and weaving, raising animals, and planting and harvesting crops.

These were the materials of instruction that inducted him into the working world. Children assisted and imitated their parents in the performance of these tasks, sometimes having a garden of their own, raising a calf, or milking cows. The boy growing up on a farm today still sees many of the overt actions in which he will participate as an adult farmer if he stays on the farm—but today nine out of ten of these boys leave for the city.

Furthermore, farming is now "agribusiness," and many important decisions of financing, accounting, planning, and marketing are only symbolic. Once the event of marketing was a simple barter or sale; now the decisions of the farmer involve a symbolic act in a symbolic market. The marketing of today bears little or no resemblance to the marketing of a hundred years ago. For example, a wheat broker may never have had his bare feet in a load of wheat, have somersaulted in the newly threshed strawstack, or chewed the gluteny wheat just before it ripened. He may never see the actual products that he buys or sells.

Many children do not really know what their fathers do. One child, asked to tell what his father did for a living, said, "He kreks." His father was a college professor and the child meant that his father corrected papers—a mystery to the child.

However, much of the instruction and learning of the child before he enters school is based on an actual performance, a direct engagement in an event. The child talks, imitates, participates, paints, dresses a doll, feeds the dog, and does hundreds of similar actions. The performance is the goal, and this performance ends the event, and begins another one. The materials of instruction are inherent in the event itself. The adults may view the performance as instructional; the child may not. The experiences engaged in are consummatory, at least for the child, and there is no implication of "going to school." Yet by the time the average child enters school he has mastered a vocabulary of some 3,000 words and also the sentence structure of English.

Unless we take home and community learning into account as we try to revolutionize the schools, we shall fail miserably. We must inquire, therefore: do we and our children live in a rich or in a poverty-stricken environment? We must remember that people are highly important elements of that environment. For example, one finding of the Coleman Report was that the verbal skills of the teacher, plus the level of education of his parents, made a measurable difference in the learning of pupils.

The intensity of an experience is a critical element in effective learning outcomes. Are children and young people fully and often intensely engaged in their school experiences or are they psychologically detached? Do they think of the school experience as something in a textbook or a recitation that is over there while they are over here? Are they spectators or participants? Learning cannot be a spectator sport.

The ratio between teacher and students is critically important as we develop curriculum programs for schools and colleges. Shall we tutor one-by-one? We tend to do this in the reading process in first grade and with remedial instruction in various fields. But since this sharply raises costs, the situations in which we use person-to-person interaction must be carefully evaluated.

The television program "Sesame Street," on the other hand, has hundreds of thousands of students per "teacher." How much instruction should be of this type? Could we increasingly use children to teach others in small groups? The conspicuous success of children in learning to speak their native language during their first six years shows the importance of personal interaction at home and with playmates. One four-year-old I know has already learned Urdu, Swahili, and English.

In later chapters this volume will discuss key factors in the development of methods and materials of instruction, and examine both theory and practice. It will raise questions and problems about learning, communication, media, and evaluation, some of which are well-known to the concerned teacher, and present other questions that probe more deeply into the issues underlying methods and materials of instruction in the educational program.

Barriers to Change

As I read the findings of sociologists and anthropologists and discuss them with friends, such as Dr. Louis Raths, three principles regarding institutions seem to receive strong consensus: (1) institutions tend to persevere in the direction in which they started; (2) institutions tend to be operated in the interests of those who run them; and (3) institutions tend to be changed by forces outside themselves. How do these principles apply to the school or college as an institution, and how do they affect the methods and materials of instruction which are used?

While we cannot deal thoroughly with these points, we should mention that schools and colleges, like other institutions, change slowly. Older friends sometimes say after visiting today's schools that they are much like the inadequate schools which they attended. Or, as the late W. S. Gray, distinguished reading specialist at the University of Chicago, once said to me: "Fifty percent of the schools are fifty years behind the times in their teaching of reading." Whether he would say that again today, I do not know.

The general high school curriculum also resembles that of fifty years or more ago. The chief bill of fare consists of foreign languages, four years of English, two years of mathematics, plus some science and social studies. The curriculum is geared to the upper half of the class, and special *ad hoc* programs are set up to meet the needs of what I shall call "the forgotten third."

The chief teaching method relies upon textbooks or lectures. The tests do not measure ability to think or to solve real problems, but only ability to remember facts long enough to pass an examination on them. As in college classrooms of fifty years ago, professors are lecturing chiefly to students who do not actively respond, but dutifully copy down the professors' words in their notebooks.

Interestingly enough, the professional schools of the university are likely to be experimenting with real-life experiences, with new media of communication, and with completely revised materials of instruction. The student in these schools is becoming an active, independent learner.

But institutions are being forced to change, and some changes are underway. For example, on the campus of The Ohio State University major curriculum revisions are being made in medicine, veterinary medicine, pharmacy, and some phases of teacher education. Audio-tutorial instruction is used in the teaching of biology, agronomy, and other subjects. Certain graduate courses in education make extensive use of real-life situations and situations developed through film, role playing, and other simulation devices. I predict that this decade of the seventies will see far greater change in instructional methods and materials than we have ever had in any decade of our educational history. This book will describe and evaluate some of these planned changes as well as some already underway.

Does it seem that this call for an accelerated evolution has placed an almost impossible burden on teachers and administrators, and has given them far more to do than they can possibly accomplish? If so, let me suggest six sources of additional assistance.

Catalysis—A catalytic agent causes changes by just being there, and sometimes the teacher's presence alone makes things happen. We all remember the heart-warming presence of persons who were miraculously at hand by chance when we needed them. But we should remember also that, as Pasteur said, "Chance favors the prepared mind."

Synergy—This word, from the Greek word *synergein,* literally means to work together, to cooperate. The elements operating in a synergistic situation combine so that the whole is more than the sum of its parts: two and two make five. The learner gets compound interest on his intellectual capital.

Symbiosis—This is living together for mutual benefit. It is likely that we are missing the symbiotic, synergistic effect that occurs when teachers and pupils, or teachers and teachers begin to work thoughtfully with each other. An ecological balance is created.

Critical mass—This is broadly defined as the least amount of fissionable material necessary to start a chain reaction. Here we need to think about developing highly generative experiences that are multiplicative rather than additive in their effect. Some of these experiences may be intense, deeply moving, or dramatic.

Heurism—This involves the Eureka effect: "I have found it!" The heuristic teacher does not attempt to find *all* the answers for the students but helps them discover many for themselves. We cannot and should not even try to find out everything by ourselves, and we can push the discovery method too hard. But certainly we can help students discover much more than our present methods and materials of instruction now reveal.

Serendipity—We find a serendipity without looking for it; it is a kind of bonus given for tending to our business— nice things happen to us. Some of our important discoveries —Roentgen rays, for example—came as a kind of happy accident. With adequate planning we should be able to get high rates of return on our investment in ideas.

"We live in two worlds," Renan says, "one dying, the other not yet born." The world that is dying is provincial, parochial, and loaded with prejudice. The other world, still in its infancy, is global, universal, and humane. Today the world has become a physical unit, but is not yet a political, spiritual, or economic one. The nation-state is out of date. If we see the world as a globe and the globe as our home, we can be hopeful about the future. If we see the world, however, only through the eyes of our home town, our home state, or nation, then our world troubles will worsen, and before long will get out of hand.

If the world is to be a good home for everybody, then revolutionary changes are needed. To change our society requires sharply improved schools, colleges, and media of communication. Just as scientific research helped create the difficulties we are now in, so research and revolutionary forms of communication can produce needed corrective changes. This book suggests ways to improve the methods and materials of instruction. Some of the ways are old, and some are new; all are worth discussion.

In a time of widespread cynicism and feelings of hopelessness, my thesis is a simple one: there is a future and we can create it. I agree with William Faulkner's comment in 1949 upon receiving the Nobel Prize for Literature:

> I decline to accept the end of man. I believe that man will not merely endure: he will prevail . . . because he has a soul, a spirit capable of compassion and sacrifice and endurance. The poet's, the writer's duty is to write about these things. It is his privilege to help man endure by lifting his heart, by reminding him of courage and honor and hope and pride and compassion and pity and sacrifice which have been the glory of his past.

As we develop sharply improved instructional experiences, we should remember that man not only has an intellect, but that his ideas can be deeply tinged with emotion. There is such a thing as "passionate intelligence." Man is both tough-minded and tender-hearted, durable and compassionate. I believe that men and women can learn the arts, skills, and attitudes required to take charge of their own lives; in fact, they often do so with distinction.

This book aims to illuminate some of the problems of developing the individual and collective virtue that helps men to endure and to prevail. But this will require a far higher level of communication than we have had in the past. It requires a revolutionary approach to improved media, methods, and materials of instruction. Are we up to it? It would be sad indeed if the epitaph of this generation should read: they knew the way but they lacked the will.

To create a future in which power and respect are shared will require marked social and individual changes. The young people of today will be the chief agents in this long-continuing task. Are they willing to accept the rigorous discipline necessary to make these changes? If so, what Herculean labors do they wish to perform? What share would they like to have in making their dreams of the future a reality? Clearly, all of us must work together to create the future because, as inventor Charles Kettering once pointed out, "We will have to spend the rest of our lives there."

CHAPTER II

The Environment Affects Learning

I noted in Chapter I that our society is in deep trouble. We are producing powerful ideas faster than we can distribute and incorporate them, and our educational programs are thrown off balance by new inventions and new demands. Parents and students want more from the schools. There is an increasing concern for accountability. We ask, therefore, whether we can design an educative environment which will enable us to develop and use ideas much more efficiently and effectively than we now do. Consequently, key issues have arisen regarding the importance of methods and materials of instruction in creating revolutionary educational change. Here are some of these issues.

Should we put our emphasis on developing persons to meet this continuing crisis, or put our time and effort into creating new materials of instruction? Obviously this is not an either/or choice. We should and must do both, but we face priorities of time and money. Buckminster Fuller, the designer-architect-scientist-philosopher, writing in *Saturday Review*, Nov. 12, 1966, said:

It is possible to design environments within which the

child will be neither frustrated nor hurt, yet free to develop spontaneously and fully without trespassing on
others. I have learned to undertake reform of the environment and not to try to reform Man. *If we design
the environment properly*, it will permit child and man to
develop safely and to behave logically.

Winston Churchill put it this way: "We shape our dwellings, and afterwards our dwellings shape us."

The Proper Educational Environment

Let us see what happens when we try to "design the
environment properly." By environment I mean all of the
surrounding conditions and influences that affect personal development. The educational environment of an
individual cannot be determined exactly by his material
surroundings. It is what one interacts with that is important, and one may react directly and concretely, or in-
directly and symbolically. The instructional environment,
then, is an interacting situation in which the continuity
of experience and the relating of experience are critically
important. At its highest level, the subject matter for
learning involves a creative interaction between the
stimulus and the individual's response.

Is certain subject matter better than others for stimulating this creative interaction? John Dewey has said:

> It is not the subject *per se* that is educative or that is
> conducive to growth. . . . There is no such thing as edu-
> cational value in the abstract. . . . The principle of inter-
> action makes it clear that failure of adaptation of material
> to needs and capacities of individuals may cause an ex-
> perience to be noneducative quite as much as failure of
> an individual to adapt himself to the material.

Two approaches, therefore, are needed—the adapting
of the individual to the materials and the adapting of
the materials to the individual, two interacting processes
for creating an educative environment.

A central problem in all societies is the extent to
which the environment in general is a learning environment. How well are we now learning? Are we moving

forward on a rising curve, or are we stuck on a plateau? What are the best circumstances under which to develop continuing learning, to keep us on a rising curve, and to build a learning community?

We can quickly describe the broad outlines for such continuous learning. The social context in which the individual is living is critically important. It makes a difference whether he is living in a village in India, cut off from most of the events of the day, or whether he is living in an affluent city where he witnesses continuing clashes of ideas. It makes a difference whether he lives in a backward-looking social context or in one of hope for a meaningful future. It makes a difference whether he is living in a slum or an affluent suburb.

During the past fifty years, the expectations of people throughout the world have been rising. Through radio, television, and picture magazines they know what life is like in Europe and North America, and they want a piece of it. So do persons living in the slums of the inner cities. They know that their children might become able business men, lawyers, doctors, and famous athletes, and they want schools and colleges that will help make these dreams come true.

It makes a difference whether one is living on a challenging frontier, such as the physical frontier faced by the pioneers who moved west from the eastern seaboard. It makes a difference whether one's family has established a tradition of attending college or whether one grows up in a family where neither the father or mother went beyond the eighth grade. Studies show that the best readers were read to as children and have many books to read at home.

It makes a difference whether teachers and administrators feel that their schools are on an intellectual and social frontier or whether they are merely struggling to keep their heads above water, with little hope of revolutionary change. It makes a difference whether young people grow up feeling that they live in a society that values human personality and provides shared power and shared respect, or in a society that thwarts curiosity, ambition, inventiveness, and creativity.

In a rich, educational environment, everyone has access to excellence. This requires a further definition. Cultural excellence has been defined by Matthew Arnold as "acquainting ourselves with the best that has been known and said in the world." Excellence also resides in people, and I would define the best people as those who put more into this society than they take out. Hopefully, many of these best people are teachers. The best in instructional materials means excellent learning resources centers, the opportunity to read, view, and listen to the best, and ready access to all the varied media.

But the best may be available and we may have the right to use it but lack the necessary study skills to use and absorb it. Libraries are of little help unless we can not only read but read critically. Excellent radio programs can be tuned in, but we may not know how to listen thoughtfully and critically. We have superb museums in all states and cities—historical, art, science, and industrial—but many parents and teachers make inadequate use even of the local ones.

One reason for our ineffective use of available excellence is that we have seen the school, home, and community as separate institutions, not as interrelated systems for learning. We need to bring all our educational resources under the umbrella of the learning community. We need to build a system of education where *everyone is in school and school is everywhere*. In a learning community, all its members have learned how to learn and have developed a taste for learning.

Criticisms of Schools Today

Let us look at some current criticisms of schools and see how these relate directly to methods and materials of instruction. Ralph Tyler, for example, has criticized the productivity of the college: "We now know enough about the conditions which contribute to learning to double the productivity of the college years." Furthermore, the development of new technologies has provided resources for teacher and student which seem likely to increase markedly the efficiencies of the efforts of both.

A visit to most schools will show that time is wasted. Students waste time by rereading material which should have been simple enough to understand with one reading. Teachers could save students' time and improve reading efficiency by selecting and teaching key terms for various subject fields. A carefully programmed course of study in vocabulary development would raise average vocabulary by as much as 10 percent—a revolutionary gain in productivity.

Philip W. Jackson, too, has been a critic of the schools, although a sympathetic one. In *Life in Classrooms* he speaks of school life as characterized by "delay, denial, interruption, and social distraction. Each is produced, in part, by the crowded conditions of the classroom."

Jackson goes on to point out that the school has "a hidden curriculum which each student (and teacher) must master if he is to make his way satisfactorily through the school." These are the social demands as contrasted with the academic demands of the school. He speaks of honoring institutional conformity instead of intellectual progress:

> The point is simply that in schools, as in prisons, good behavior pays off. . . . Curiosity, as an instance, that most fundamental of all scholarly traits, is of little value in responding to the demands of conformity. The curious person typically engages in a kind of probing, poking, and exploring that is almost antithetical to the attitude of the passive conformist.

If the curriculum, the teachers, and the system itself reward curiosity and creativity, then we will prepare and use materials and methods of instruction to achieve these purposes. However, if the rewards are chiefly for superior, uncritical memorizing of what the book or teacher says, then memorizing will become the accepted behavior.

This is not a plea for uncritical rewarding of non-conformity. Nonconformity can be both rational and irrational, and conformity can be wise as well as stupid. Further, one cannot be a successful reformer unless he knows what the previous reforms were. George Santayana has pointed out that "those who cannot remember the past are condemned to repeat it."

Fields of Instruction

The kinds of instruction carried on in the school will depend not only on the purposes of the school or college but also on the purposes of our society. In many of the educational programs of the past, a central need has been for developing persons who can keep our industrial society increasingly productive. Business schools of fifty or seventy-five years ago provided the needed book-keepers, accountants, stenographers, typists, and so on, and that need continues to be emphasized in the high school curriculum. For example, present technology requires sales people, clerical workers, and stenographers —hence the demand for courses such as distributive education.

But the critical problems of American society are no longer chiefly technological; they are also cultural problems of values and outlooks, and of thoughtful consuming as well as efficient producing. Hence the need is increasingly for workers who can think and meet the new demands placed upon us by technology. The trained worker may be technically literate but aesthetically, economically, and politically illiterate in the sense that he lacks thoughtfulness, future-mindedness, and a deep concern about the way society is moving.

On this issue we have both heartening and discouraging data. The discouraging data show clearly that there is vast ignorance on matters affecting the whole society. On the other hand, the Gallup Poll has shown that on certain matters the 18-year-olds are the best informed group in the nation. In short, those just graduating from high school have, whatever their weaknesses, current information not possessed by large numbers of average Americans.

Another key point in dealing with materials of instruction is the realization that all experiences have side-effects; there are concomitant learnings. If one is learning no more than he is studying, something is wrong. If he learns to read but does not like to read, what good is it? Dewey said, "The most important attitude that can be formed is that of desire to go on learning."

External and Internal Environments

Much of our thinking about instructional experiences assumes that they are stimuli from the outside. Change these external stimuli by improved materials of instruction, we assume, and we shall have sharp gains in learning. But we fail to see that the internal and external environments are interacting, and that unless we are aware of the internal environment we cannot perceive the external environment thoughtfully and analytically.

The environment of the home and community is increasingly seen as a key factor in continuing learning; it makes a difference in those experiences and attitudes which the student brings with him to school. These experiences include those with parents, one's own age-mates, and with books, newspapers, radio, television, or other media-guided experiences within the community. We shall not successfully meet the problem of educating the inner city children unless we set up an active program of co-operation with parents.

Obviously, greater opportunity to change the external environment comes at more mature stages of learning. The way in which our internal environment responds to the incoming stimulus is what determines the nature of the stimulus. One cannot perceive something unless he first conceives it, even in a sketchy way. He cannot really learn something unless he already partly "knows" it.

A book, even a classic, may "turn off" one child and another one on. But a gifted teacher, writer, or speaker may excite his audience with an explanation of a current event, an excellent book or play, or a new topic in a textbook. The approach of the teacher may determine the depth or the shallowness of student reaction to an instructional situation. In a real sense, our environment is what we make it.

We are all aware of selective attention. But the counterpart of selective attention is selective inattention. This inattention may occur merely because we cannot pay attention to everything at once. It may also occur because the individual shuns an experience or turns it off, or it may occur because we have provided no rich introductory experiences in a field of instruction.

What is an Educative Environment?

Benjamin Bloom points out in *Stability and Change* that specialists "are able to specify some of the major characteristics of an environment which will positively or negatively affect the development of general intelligence or school achievement." He says, for example:

> Differences in general intelligence are likely to be related to:
>
> 1. Stimulation provided in the environment for verbal development.
>
> 2. Extent to which affection and reward are related to verbal-reasoning accomplishments.
>
> 3. Encouragement of active interaction with problems, exploration of the environment, and the learning of new skills.

He also says:

> Differences in school achievement are likely to be related to:
>
> 1. Meaning which education comes to have for one's personal advancement and role in society.
>
> 2. Level of education of and value placed on education by the significant adults in the individual's life.
>
> 3. Extent to which school achievement is motivated

and reinforced by parents or significant adults in the individual's life.

The development of the stimulating and responsive environments that Bloom suggests is central in preparing all materials and methods of instruction. New methods of teaching and superbly produced materials can profoundly affect the instructional process and markedly change the intellectual and emotional climate of teaching and learning. But to make the needed revolutionary change we need an overall instructional design and a system governed by this design. All effective education is "programmed" in some degree, sometimes by the learner himself.

Today the school and college pay most attention to the cognitive, the intellectual, side of life. We forget that all experiences have in some degree a preferential or valuing element. Feeling is sometimes more important than knowing, and may vitally affect what we know. We typically do not provide rich, aesthetic experiences in art, music, theater, film, and drama, experiences described by Dewey as "intensifications of the ordinary." We have many tests of whether information has been "learned," but few tests of the long-term effects of those experiences which may touch us deeply, which strongly influence our ideas of right and wrong, and our speculations as to who we are and the role we could play in this world.

The methods and materials of instruction should deal with all categories of behavior: knowing, feeling, and doing. We have tended to neglect the feeling environment in which children and young people live. One teacher in a suburban school told her seventh grade class at their first meeting: "I'm either going to break you or you are going to break me, and I can tell you right now that you are not going to break me." This teacher saw the students as enemies or semirebellious troops engaged in a war which the teacher proposed to win.

Some teachers believe that failure and low grades have a disciplinary and therapeutic effect. They say, "You will experience failure in life, and so you must get ready for it in school." Wiser teachers say, "You will be successful in life—therefore my job is to get you ready for it." A ninth grade biology teacher told her class, "No one will get an A in the first six weeks' grading." In short, no matter how hard they worked, an A was unattainable.

Some learning environments are friendly, supportive, optimistic, and energizing. Others are cold, threatening, pessimistic, and enervating. Bloom's statement about "affection and reward" as critical environmental variables needs to be underlined in all our concerns with appropriate methods and materials of instruction. Some learning environments encourage dependence; some, independence. Some train, others educate.

The experiences of becoming independent and responsible, of growing up, are deeply rooted in our inner selves. For example, the question: what did Thoreau say about the person who marches to a different drummer? (an information question) might be a prelude to the question: are *you* marching to a distant drum? Or are you really following Omar Khayyam's advice:

> Ah, take the Cash, and let the Credit go,
> Nor heed the rumble of a distant Drum?

What we ask for in our educational programs are those experiences which both socialize and individualize, those which make us both cooperating members of a group and also provide for idiosyncracies (literally one's own mixing together). There are times to go along with others and times to blaze new trails. There are times to say "yes" and proceed, and there are times to say "no" and stand firm.

Sometimes we need to see ourselves as working members in a synergistic, cooperative enterprise; sometimes we see ourselves as unique ends—like no one else in the world. In his book *On Knowing* Jerome S. Bruner speaks of thinking as "an inner colloquy patterned by early external dialogues." We speak to ourselves so that we can speak to others; we speak to others so that we can learn how to talk to ourselves and continue the inner colloquy, a kind of ongoing feedback.

To instruct, then, we must help students develop a dialogue between their external and internal inputs, the external environment and the internal environments. Sometimes we overemphasize the external stimuli—books, study trips, pictures, photographs, and so on—and underemphasize the internal stimuli—our thoughts and reactions. Thoreau was concerned with the fit between his inner and outer environment when he said, "I went to the woods because I wished to live deliberately, to front only the essential facts of life, and see if I could not learn what it had to teach, and not, when I came to die, discover that I had not lived."

Our aim in school and college is to learn how to live by thinking, by facing the essentials, and by discovering (like Thoreau) whether we are really living or merely existing. Actually, the mental, spiritual, and emotional environment in which we live is one which we usually take for granted, and, therefore, are least likely to examine. However, unless we examine this internal environment, we cannot adequately, thoughtfully, and analytically perceive the external environment.

A Self-Examination

Socrates said that the unexamined life is not worth living. Yet we are fearful about examining the things which we hold most dear. We might discover, as Dewey pointed out in 1930, that we may have a "fear of fear itself." What might such an examination reveal about the kind of educational program we believe in and the kind of environment of instructional experiences we would aim for?

First, the examination would reveal inconsistencies. It would disclose that if we believe *this,* we cannot believe *that.* If we believe that all persons everywhere should have a chance to develop their potential, then we cannot segregate ourselves, our families, and our schools from the lives of other persons. We cannot believe deeply in superior

schools for our own children unless we also believe in superior schools for all children. Dewey put it this way:
"What the best and wisest parent wants for his own child,
that must the community want for all of its children."

Second, a self-examination might reveal that we don't
really believe some of the things that we thought we believed. Do we believe that we ought to do something for
the poor, the dispossessed, and the underprivileged? This
attitude sounds like a wise, unselfish one, but it is a one-
way approach. Many persons do not want anyone to do
something for them. There is an anticolonial attitude throughout the world today because people do not trust those
who do things *for* them but are unwilling to do things
with them.

Are our curriculum materials set up so that teachers
can do things with students instead of for them? Or better
still, are they set up so that children and young people
can do something for themselves with only limited teacher
assistance? A family is markedly changed when parents are
eager to have their children do many things for themselves.
Several persons working on instructional materials of a
new type have told me that some teachers will not let
the children do things by themselves. These teachers keep
thinking "little children can't do this," so they oversupervise
their students. We might revolutionize our schools and colleges if we accepted and carried out as our basic aim the
continued maturing of children and their growing independence.

Third, a critical self-examination would reveal our
general attitude toward what is likely to happen to us in
the future. Are we governed by our fears or by our best
hopes? Would a friendly critic see us as basically negative,
hopeless, and cynical, or as positive, hopeful, and optimistic?
Would he find that we believe we are in charge of
our own lives, or that unpredictable social forces have us
in their power? If we feel that we can change ourselves
and our environment, we shall have one kind of curriculum.
But if teachers are fearful, and do not believe that children

can be trusted, then we will get another kind of curriculum.

Perhaps more than we realize, our present curriculum is based on the fear of poor discipline, the fear of possible lack of control. As a consequence, we build a curriculum that emphasizes teacher domination and provides many overt and covert punishments for children who step out of line. The punishment may create a continuing anxiety about failing in the future.

How can we create the attractive learning environment which nearly all of us seek but which appears to be so elusive? There are no easy answers to this tough problem, but I shall present my experiences and views of ways of meeting these problems through new and old approaches to materials and methods of instruction. This can be a long bill of particulars including a large number of problems to be attacked and "solved." It is so large that we must break it down into its major components if we wish to be realistic about reform. Further, we must set priorities dependent on time, personnel, funds, and goals.

As we look more deeply into the instructional process we see that three components are involved: the learner, the teacher, and the instructional methods and materials themselves. Two of these factors are persons, and the third involves the interaction of persons with materials. How much can each of these factors be changed or re-arranged to achieve stated purposes? Or do we have a built-in personal and institutional inflexibility which is changed only with great effort?

First we have the learner who brings a background of information, attitudes, and skills—an input to the learning situation. He also brings with him his perceiving and con-ceptualizing methodology. He is learning how to put exper-iences together to produce generalizations, principles, and concepts. During the instructional interaction we hope that he will add to, change, refile, reclassify, and reorganize his experiences. We assume that teachers can significantly change some of these personal characteristics of the learner by using varied instructional materials more effectively.

Second, we have the teacher who brings to the instructional interaction his knowledge and competency in the subject under study. He brings his concept of the role of a teacher. Hopefully, he brings the experiences of an educated man to the instructional process; we want him to teach not only what he knows, but more important, what he is. The richer his background and the greater his sensitivity to the background of his students, the more interaction, and hence the more significant the instructional outcomes can be. A key role of a teacher can be that of a diagnostician, a prescriber and organizer of suggested experiences, and an evaluator of instructional outcomes.

Third, there is the input from the instructional materials, the planned (and unplanned) experiences with which the student will interact. Some of these experiences will involve the communication skills of reading and writing, speaking and listening, and visualizing and observing. There will be plans for getting the rich, first-hand experiences so necessary for building attitudes and concepts. The teacher's role at this point is critical, since he can help the student organize and mentally file his own unrelated, isolated experiences, thus making them retrievable for further use. The instructor can also help provide a "cafeteria" of instructional materials from which the learner can make choices based on formal and informal diagnoses. Unfortunately, most schools and colleges do not yet provide such diagnoses or instructional materials centers.

Buckminster Fuller was quoted at the beginning of this chapter as saying, "If we design the environment properly, it will permit child and man to develop safely and to behave logically." We do not have many persons whom we call environmental designers, yet Fuller's concept is a fruitful and lively one. In the remaining chapters of the book we shall look more closely at ways in which to create and develop the ideas, skills, and attitudes so necessary for meaningful instruction.

CHAPTER III

Toward Universal Communication

One of the great movements now sweeping the entire world is fueled by the idea that everyone should have access to the excellence now available only to a minority of the world's population. But clearly the persons with limited education cannot now share in this bounty of excellence. James Harvey Robinson, writing in 1923 in his *Humanizing of Knowledge,* pointed out the grave need to put knowledge into a form understandable to the average person, the common man. Robinson himself could translate important, complicated ideas into clear and interesting prose. He was a superb communicator in the sense of communicating to share ideas and feelings in a mood of mutuality.

The sharing of ideas and feelings in the fields of health, economics, government, literature, aesthetics, or ecology requires simply written materials with specific readers in mind. It requires extensive use of all media—including radio, recordings, films, exhibits, and opportunities to travel. In the United States, material written at the twelfth grade level will be understood by only half of its adult readers, because only half of our population over twenty-five years of age has had twelve years of schooling. To be understood by three-fourths of the people, one must write at the eighth grade level. However, this is not a highly limiting reading level; most important ideas can be made understandable to persons with eight years of schooling.

Too many textbooks, pamphlets, encyclopedias and other reference volumes are written at a grade level above that of the readers for whom they were prepared. In most classes at or above the fifth grade level reading competencies will range from second grade to eighth grade. A text for children in the eighth grade should be written at the seventh grade level to reach 80 percent of the class members. Readability formulas—for example, Dale-Chall, Flesch, Fry, Gunning, Klare, Lorge, Spache, and Taylor—should be used to test the reading levels.

Considerable material written by specialists also must be rewritten for the reading level of a layman. Here are some examples of ways in which a manuscript has been or might be edited to make it more easily comprehensible:

Original

The English language, as being the offspring of two parent languages very different in form and spirit, and having been in no inconsiderable degree modified in its growth by influences from various other tongues, contains, as was inevitable, very many anomalies; and in no particular are these anomalies more numerous and striking than in its orthography, with the single exception, perhaps, of its orthoepy.

—Third Edition of *Webster's Collegiate Dictionary* (1928)

Revision

English is the offspring of two parent languages different in form and spirit. It has been considerably changed and influenced by other languages, and thus contains many irregularities. It is strikingly irregular in spelling and even more so in pronunciation.

Original

It is sometimes alleged that a complete system of social security would ultimately have the effect of discouraging self-reliance and even fostering unemployment by destroying the incentives to industry, by removing the rough but salutary influence of discipline.

Revision

Some say that if you guaranteed persons jobs and an old age pension that they would get lazy, lose their self-respect, and not want to work. They also say that if you're not afraid of losing your job you won't keep on your toes.

Certain proverbs, if rewritten in academic textbook style, would become clumsy and weak. "I came, I saw, I conquered" would become "I arrived at my destination. I perceived the situation. I subjugated the opposing forces." "All that glitters is not gold" is easy to understand. The academic revision would be: "It is not inappropriate to know that all articles which coruscate do not necessarily possess a high intrinsic value." "Early to bed and early to rise, makes a man healthy, wealthy, and wise" would be changed to "Early retirement is a significant factor in one's physical development, pecuniary success, and intellectual stature."

Today we are developing programs dealing with "the right to read." Many of these programs aim to improve reading skills, but we have neglected and overlooked the idea that the right to read requires readable materials. If children and young people cannot easily read the textbooks and other instructional materials prepared for them, then learning to decode or to pronounce words is not the central need of the learner. What we must do is to provide textbooks and other materials at the reading level of the learner. We can use reading lists such as those prepared by the American Library Association which indicate the grade reading level of the book. If we know the reading level of the prospective reader we can match the book to his level. More readable instructional materials will enable the student to move more easily through the material and with greater enjoyment.

It is also difficult to communicate, to share ideas, because we often mishear, misread, and misobserve: "I had to bear the *blunt* of it" or "This fellow *lashed* on to me and I couldn't get rid of him." A patient reported her doctor diagnosed her illness as "sick-as-hell" anemia (sickle cell). A child may say, "I was all *puckered* out." "Mitigate" is confused with "militate" both in the press and in official reports.

The specialist not only does not realize that the layman often possesses a low level of technical information, but he prefers to use prestigious, polysyllabic words, more technical than necessary. A plumber once wrote a research bureau asking whether hydrochloric acid could be safely used to clean out sewer pipes. The first written reply was as follows: "The efficacy of hydrochloric acid is indisputable, but the corrosive residue is incompatible with metallic permanence."

The plumber then thanked the bureau for this information approving his procedure. The dismayed research bureau wrote again, saying, "We cannot assume responsibility for the production of toxic and noxious residue with hydrocholoric acid and suggest you use an alternative procedure." Once more the plumber thanked them for their approval. Finally, the bureau, worried about the New York sewers, called in a third scientist who wrote: "Don't use hydrochloric acid. It eats hell out of the pipes."

The teacher of English may be unaware that many of her high school students think that "canst" means "can't," and that "supersede" means to be "better than." It is difficult for her to realize that they do not know the difference between "interment" and "internment," "ingenious" and "ingenuous," "venal" and "venial," and "arraign" and "arrange." An able high school teacher of social studies once told me that most high school juniors in the school where she taught would know the meaning of "interdict"; a test, however, showed that most did not.

In the past, we have overdone the "heavy" textbook style of writing. Today, the use of paperbacks and pamphlets in schools and colleges provides a simpler, more informal style. The following suggestions for such writing are used by the able journalist writing for the average reader. Where appropriate, I have made suggestions regarding the preparation of comprehensible audio-visual materials.

1. *Define your audience and purpose*

If you are writing a pamphlet on financial security to be read by nearly all adults, you must ask two questions: What do they *want* to know? What do they *need* to know? You must start with what people want to know in order to build a background for what they need to know. You must get into the reader's shoes and think and feel as he does, and be as ignorant or as knowledgeable as he is. This is not easy.

A friend once gave me directions for reaching his summer cottage. I wrote down what he said and even phoned him to confirm his overcomplicated instructions. He gave me many details I did not need to know. These simple directions would have been enough: Get on route 25 at Gorham, Maine. Stay on 25 till you see a blinker light at the Shell station three miles past Center Harbor. Turn left. Go straight ahead for eight miles till you come to a causeway to an island. Cross the causeway. Take the first graveled road to the left. Drive four miles to the end of the road. Turn left through the white pillars and watch for our sign, about one-half mile down the road.

The "key points" in a set of directions are the places where the stranger may go wrong. Key points are critical in all communication. We do not need to tell the person more than he needs to know; he needs only to know the decision points.

Every message contains "directions" of some kind. But why do most people who give directions finish by saying, "You can't miss it"? They think their directions are clear, but they are clear only because they already know how to get there. Hence the "COIK fallacy"—clear only if known.

Similarly, the instructions for assembling a "knocked-down" piece of furniture are often inadequate. Obviously, however, the man who wrote the instructions knew how to assemble it.

What is your own purpose in preparing instructional material? Do you have five or six key ideas for example, that everyone ought to know about financial security? What do you want the reader to feel and do about this problem? Is your concern chiefly a cognitive, informational change to master a few important facts? A change in attitude or opinion? A change in skills such as driving a car?

2. Avoid a lengthy introduction

Speakers have often been advised that if they do not strike oil in the first five minutes, they should stop boring. Many introductions are both dull and useless. An editor of an education journal told me that he can usually eliminate a page of introductory material in a manuscript. If introductions are too long, the reader may give up before he gets to the first point. Use a short introduction, if any, to make clear what is coming, the questions that will be answered. This will also help to sharpen the logic of the material.

Brevity is not only the soul of wit, it is also the essence of good communication. The thirty-minute film should have been only half as long. The long-winded speaker does not realize that his speech did not get across. He should have quit when he was ahead, but he added more and more. As a short speech it would have been excellent; as a long speech it was a bore. The poor speaker quits when he is tired. The good speaker, like the good writer or film maker, quits just before the audience gets tired.

The amateur worries about what he is going to put in his speech, article, or videotape. The expert worries about what he should take out and follows the rule: if in doubt, take it out. An artistic performance is concentrated and has a central focus. Lincoln spoke for less than two minutes at Gettysburg, but his message still tugs at the heart. "Fiddle-dee-dee," a delightful film produced by the Canadian Film Board, is only three minutes long. "A Word In Your Ear," produced by the National Association of Educational Broadcasters, compresses rich meaning into a recording of twenty minutes.

Winston Churchill asked his staff to confine memoranda to one page. A president of a large corporation wrote a letter to his ten vice-presidents suggesting that their letters and memoranda were often too long. The next morning he had on his desk nine letters bearing only the single word: "Right!" The tenth letter merely said: "Right on!"

But sometimes messages can be too brief and too concentrated. A summary prepared by someone else may be of little value unless we have had the first-hand experiences from which the summary was developed. No one can get an education reading or viewing summaries; they lack illuminating concreteness. Here we must face two important demands relating to amount of detail used in writing. Aristotle said, "Don't go into more detail than the occasion warrants." And William James warned, "You cannot see any farther into a generalization than your knowledge of its details extends." In short, details are important but do not overdo it.

3. Tell a logical story

Study your key points and note the basic arguments and ideas being presented. Are the big ideas clearly outlined and developed, or are they hidden? Could a reader easily remember them and tell them to someone else? Is there a logic that is applied to chronology, cause and effect, and so on?

Here we face a difficult task in preparing instructional materials. The logic of the specialist and the logical structure of a mature subject may not be the best basis for teaching this material to inexperienced or immature persons. They need a psychological approach which may differ from the structure used by the specialist. A psychological approach will meet the learner on his level of growth. John Dewey put it this way in *Democracy and Education:*

> Educationally, it has to be noted that logical characteristics of method, since they belong to subject matter which has reached a high degree of intellectual elaboration, are different from the method of the learner—the chronological order of passing from a cruder to a more refined intellectual quality of experience.

4. *Make your key points visible*

A reader should be able to skim an article or a chapter, determine quickly what it says, and decide whether to read it in detail. It furnishes him with an outline or filing system for the ideas to be learned. Therefore, visual guides can make the pamphlet or book clearer and more inviting. Sometimes you can help the reader with subheads, italics, boldface, or by numbering the points made. You can spread your material out typographically and make it less dense in appearance by more paragraphing or by adding more space between lines. "Aerate" your material, let it breathe, and let the white paper show up more. In addition, some kinds of type are more readable than others.

5. *Communicate* net. *Be concise but clear*

Maybe you have covered too much in one article or film. It is better to fully uncover one point than to try to cover ten. Do not try to cover the ground; uncover it. Make the article, book, or recording as long as it needs to be, no longer. The popularity of proverbs or quotations is often due to their crisp and easily remembered wording. Note these comments from Oscar Wilde's *The Picture of Dorian Gray:*

> . . . the value of an idea has nothing whatsoever to do with the sincerity of the man who expresses it.
>
> I can sympathize with everything, except suffering.

He was always late on principle, his principle being
that punctuality is the thief of time.

They never have anything to say, but they say it
charmingly.

6. *Make your communication personal*

Think of writing a personal letter rather than a report.
De Quincey once said: "If you want to read drama, rob
the mails." You can make material personal by using conversation, by putting people into your story, and by using
real names and places. Notice how personal the stories
are in *Reader's Digest.* Do you nearly always read the
"Letters" column in *Time, Newsweek,* or *Life?* They are
personal, simple, and nearly everybody can read them.
Documentary films are powerful because they are intimate
and personal; we can identify with the persons portrayed.

The dividing line between impersonal reporting and
personal reporting in writing is at about the eighth
grade level. When material deals with a named person and
his problems it tends to be at this level or below. When it
deals with impersonal ideas it tends to be above the eighth
grade level.

7. *Invite reader, listener, or viewer participation and in-volvement*

All effective communication explicitly or implicitly answers the questions of the reader, viewer, or listener.
Note the effectiveness of questions and answers used in
printed radio or film interviews; our studies show that
interviews in a magazine are two or three grade levels
easier to read than the rest of the articles. Effective communication causes the individual to identify himself with,
or to involve himself with the message. Sometimes a pro-
vocative situation or problem is presented in a so-called
discussion film.

8. *Use pointed examples*

You can simplify and clarify material in a book or an

article by inserting examples that provide the concrete detail that William James suggested was imperative. Many highly condensed explanations in books, pamplets, and articles need illustrations. These may include anecdotes, a more concrete explanation, or an illustration which makes an abstract idea concrete. Textbook writers sometimes say: "The reader will think of other examples." This usually means that he has run out of them himself. Most graduate students, when asked to give an example of oxidation, say the rusting of iron. Few point out that all of us are slowly oxidizing—burning up. Season writing with anecdotes. Amplify by examples; in short, "examplify."

9. *Simplify the vocabulary*

Avoid pedantic mumbo-jumbo. You can sometimes substitute short, simple, vivid, easily understood words for the longer Latin or Greek equivalents. Instead of "confronting" problems, just face them. A *sine qua non* is merely a "necessity." A "multifaceted" problem is "many-sided." We have too many "facets;" why not say "phase" or "aspect"? Do not "proceed on the assumption"; just "assume." Instead of saying, "It would be impossible for me to do it," why not say, "I can't do it"?

Avoid polysyllabic pseudo-profundity which may dazzle but not illuminate. There is no need to dress up the obvious in the finery of the obscure. However, when important and difficult technical words are needed, explain them or put them into a context which suggests their meaning without insulting the intelligence of the able reader. People like to learn new, hard words, so do not rob them of this unexpected bonus, this enjoyable serendipity. Important hard or technical terms might well be planfully repeated throughout a book. Planned duplication is important.

10. *Use audio-visual material of various kinds*

Simple drawings, graphs, maps, and photographs may sharpen the material, but avoid using them without a clear-cut purpose. You do not usually need a picture of an apple when you write about apples, but you do need color pictures to depict the many varieties of apples. A map or diagram may do pictorially what is hard to do with words alone. However, many maps, charts, and diagrams are too complicated and may need simplifying. An engraving should not be used as a poster. Clarification, not decoration, is the aim.

11. *Repeat and summarize thoughtfully*

As you approach the end of your writing you should be answering the reader's questions: So what? What is the author driving at? Do not leave the reader up in the air when he has finished reading. When the article or chapter is long, the reader will forget points made earlier so carry key points along with you; do not drop them abruptly. When you reach the third or fourth points in a long communication, you might remind the reader what the first and second ones were. In a long article, a summary may recast the key points that have been made, but tell them in a fresh way. Mere repetition is not good enough.

I have discussed chiefly reading and writing. The same points could be made about motion pictures, television, radio, and exhibits. No matter what medium is used, our objective is that stated by H. G. Wells in his *Outline of History:* "We have still to insure . . . that all that can be thought and known is kept plainly, honestly, and easily available to the ordinary men and women who are the substance of mankind." This is a good principle to follow in developing materials of instruction.

There is a science and an art of communication. The principles or "rules" here presented may be helpful up to a point. Certainly they can be used to make all communications clearer, hence more comprehensible. But if to this clarity which many writers can achieve we can add the artistry and creativity of the gifted writer, film maker, or speaker, we shall have done well indeed.

CHAPTER IV

What is
Worth Knowing?

Every teacher and every producer and user of materials
of instruction must face the perennial and perplexing
question: What is worth knowing? By knowledge I mean
information, skills, and attitudes incorporated into one's
intellectual and emotional habits, mastered and retained
by continuing use. Herbert Spencer wrote a long essay,
Education: Intellectual, Moral, and Physical, on this topic
in 1860, and sociologist Robert Lynd wrote the book *Knowl-*
edge for What? in 1939. New knowledge, in particular,
is difficult to assess, and may be accepted with reluctance.
This reluctance is indicated by Spencer's inaccurate analysis
of what was happening in British schools (remember this
was in 1860):

The once universal practice of learning by rote is daily
falling into discredit. All modern authorities condemn the
old mechanical way of teaching the alphabet. The multi-
plication table is now frequently taught experimentally.
. . . The rote-system, like other systems of its age, made
more of the forms and symbols than of the things sym-

bolized. To repeat the words correctly was everything; to understand their meaning nothing. . . . Along with rote-teaching, is declining also the nearly allied teaching by rules. The particulars first, and then the generalization, is the new method. . . .

[It is still the new method today and is often violated in methods and materials of instruction.]

The learning that is of most worth enables us to get a sense of our individual and social identity—who we are, what we care about, and what we can do. This self-analysis tells us whether we are in charge of our own lives or are ruled by others, an actor or a spectator, powerful or weak, a manager or managed. It tells us whether we believe the world can be changed or whether change is impossible.

The curriculum of the school should help students attain a sense of their individual and social worth. Nearly everyone wants to be like others, yet to be different and to stand out as an individual. But many who try do not succeed, often because they do not know how. To compensate for their sense of weakness, they may set up fantasies of imagined power. Others have apocalyptic dreams of an impending revolution when the "good guys" will be in charge and the "bad guys" will get their deserved come-uppance.

Fulfillment, Discrimination, Communication

That knowledge is of most worth which enables a person to do the best that he can, to be fulfilled. The knowledge especially to be prized enables a person to live close to the upper limits of his physical, mental, and emotional powers. Few people ever reach this ideal; most live far below their potential. Unless we learn how to, invest our time, money, and energy to get maximum return, we shall find ourselves without a life of our own, or with a diminished life managed and manipulated by others. Once I chatted with a college student who was training for the annual Boston marathon. When I asked him why he wanted to run it, he replied, "It tests the limits of my endurance."

Persons with a poverty of goods and ideas have permitted their life map to be constructed by someone else. Thus today many people find themselves without real options, their choices for action severely limited. They lack elbow room; there is no scope for personal decision making, the essence of a good life. They lack the autonomy that comes with the mastery of knowledge. They become slaves to ignorance, powerless, and often apathetic. They do not call the tune; they dance to it.

That knowledge is of most worth which generates knowledge. It does this by extending what we already know, by deepening and refining it. For example, the typical eighth grade student knows the word "malaria." He may not, however, know that *mal* means "bad" and that *aria* means "air." When he learns the meaning of *mal,* he can then generate such words as maladjusted, maladroit, malady, malaise, malappropriate, malignant, and so on. Or, a small child can add hundreds of new words to his repertoire if he learns to use "-ing" and "-ed" to produce words like working, worked; talking, talked; and jumping, jumped.

Knowledge can be generated either by adding to or by making better use of what we already know. Speaking broadly, we can use an additive or an integrative approach to learning. We can read more books, listen to more lectures, and view more images—moving or still. Or we can rework or reconstruct what we already know. Obviously, we can and should use both methods.

Instead of always trying to gain more information, we might be better off to spend more time learning how to rearrange, summarize, or systematize what we already have. Good educational practice demands that students vary their methods of filing material for optimum retrieval. A skillful reader of a dictionary has already discovered that there are a limited number of excellent ways to define, limit, and file a concept. For example, we can file "dog," "cat," and "elephant" under "vertebrates" or under "animal." We can file "animal" under "quadruped," "biped," "octopod," and so on. Filing is both an art and a science. Indeed, we might well test a person not only on what he knows but also on how skillfully and critically he files, retrieves, and uses what knowledge he already possesses.

I believe that a central aim of all education is to develop an independent learner; hence that learning is most valuable which helps us develop independence. Spencer warns against "making the pupil a merely passive recipient of other's ideas" and suggests that, instead, he be led "to be an active inquirer or self-instructor."

That knowledge is of most worth that enables us to work efficiently and effectively in the organization and application of ideas. Spencer also said, "there are very few minds that become as efficient as they might be . . . the greater part of what has been acquired, being unorganized, soon drops out of recollection; what remains is mostly inert—the art of applying knowledge not having been cultivated. . . ." Philosophers Whitehead and Dewey often use the term "inert knowledge."

That knowledge is of most worth which enables us to see the wholeness of our life—the system which is at work whether we realize it or not. When we do not see the system as a whole we try to refashion some of the parts, thereby getting partial relief but postponing the time when the whole system must be studied and reflected upon.

Many studies show that additional time spent on reflection, on thinking about what we have read, heard, seen, or done, is highly profitable, hence the importance of that knowledge which helps us organize, classify, pattern, structure, rearrange, reconstruct, synthesize, and conceptualize what we know. The able teacher helps students develop connections, interactions, relationships, and patterns.

That knowledge is best which can be learned. This seem "truistic" but, applied to the curriculum of the school or college, it has significant meaning. If "to teach" always meant to help students arrange their experiences so that learning will surely result, there would be no problem.

In actual practice, however, what is taught may not be learned. A revolution in education would occur if we decided to teach only what will actually be learned. We would then be forced either to sharply change teaching methods so that learning did occur, or change the content of our present curriculum.

For example, if our aim in teaching a foreign language, is to have the student attain a certain stated level of fluency in speaking, then we would either achieve it, or change the methods or the goal. Competency in the English language, however, should take precedence over competency in a foreign language lest the student become illiterate in two languages. The most striking thing about the data in a study by Dr. John B. Carroll, then of Harvard, was the "generally low median levels of attainment in audio-lingual skills that they reveal. The median graduate with a foreign language major can speak and comprehend the language only at about a Foreign Service Institute speaking rating of '2+', that is, somewhere between a 'limited working proficiency' and a 'minimum professional proficiency' . . . One would think that the median college foreign language major ought to attain more than a 'minimum professional proficiency' in basic language skills as a result of his efforts. . . ."

That knowledge is of most worth which enables us to tell the difference between fact and opinion, evidence and propaganda, and the logical and the illogical. This means that schools and colleges need to place heavy emphasis on methods and materials of instruction in critical reading, critical listening, and critical observing. Actually the objectives of the teaching of science, history, and other subjects emphasize standards for judging acceptable evidence. Yet the typical classroom examinations given to test competence or mastery are largely tests of ability to remember information, not to judge its validity or to apply it in new situations.

When we look at or hear the phony advertisements that emphasize unthinking acceptance of unreasoned choices, we see the importance of good judgment as a major goal of education. The ever-present manipulation of individuals by word and image is a constant hazard for the consumers of all media. It is paramount, therefore, that we learn to be discriminating consumers of all messages received, either through personal communication or through communication by the mass media. Such knowledge is especially valuable in a world saturated with self-seeking propaganda.

That knowledge is of high worth which enables students to communicate effectively in reading and writing, speaking and listening, and visualizing and observing. We do not yet adequately diagnose levels of competency in these areas in order to provide needed instruction at points of strength and weakness. Let us take reading as an example (many of the same comments apply to listening and observing).

All of us agree that the ability to read is of crucial importance. But this consensus is not evident in the school and college curricula. Typically, after the sixth grade, schools assume that learning to read will be taken care of through mastery of stated subject matter. But studies show that this approach is not effective, and some of the nation's best high schools now provide continuing guidance in developing the varied and increasingly complex skills needed for reading increasingly complex materials. The work of Ellen Thomas at the University of Chicago Laboratory High School is an example; George Spache has written thoughtfully on this topic in *The Teaching of Reading*.

Many persons read everything at the same speed. They do not know how to change gears in reading or shift to skimming or slow critical reading. Further, even college students, graduate and undergraduate, usually have no lifetime reading plan. They have not read or reread from the works of Dickens, Emerson, Thoreau, Mark Twain, Thomas Hardy, H. G. Wells, Sinclair Lewis, or Robert Frost, The odyssey of *Malcolm X*, slain Negro leader, will be illuminating and helpful to many high school students. High school and college literature courses should place a high priority on helping students sample a wide range of books, magazines, and newspapers, and plan a lifetime career of thoughtful, enjoyable reading. Easily available, inexpensive paperbacks can revolutionize tastes and abilities in reading.

The mastery of knowledge is important, but this knowledge must be located before it can be mastered. In a society that sometimes changes its answers faster than it changes its questions, learning how to do reference reading is of great value. This means mastering the elementary and advanced skills of reading dictionaries, encyclopedias, and thesauri, and learning to use card catalogues and indexes of various kinds.

That knowledge is of most worth which enables us to share ideas with others. If we can read and write, we can have access to the best ideas in the world. If we can speak and listen, we can participate both in intellectual and emotional interaction with other people. If we can visualize and observe, we can exchange ideas in a nonverbal medium.

The ability to speak well and to listen thoughtfully is paramount in this society. After all, writing is often speech that has been written; reading is a form of "listening" to inner speech. Not only is it important to be a good listener, it is equally important to stimulate conversation that is worth listening to. How often do students have good discussions in class? Is it reasonable to say that knowledge which best stimulates thoughtful conversation is of great worth? The ability to ask penetrating questions is surely as important as the ability to give penetrating answers. Formal and informal programs in debating have high value in developing this ability.

Sensitivity and Awareness
That knowledge is of most worth which contributes a sense of joy, exhilaration, and poignancy to the life of the

learner. This requires in-depth experiences which develop a zest for life and the joy of discovery (the Eureka effect) as a continuing accompaniment to a life richly lived. In this respect, we must ask when the student should have immediate, first-hand "sense" knowledge and when he should depend chiefly on knowledge mediated through semiconcrete or symbolic experiences. Do we want students to know, or to know about? When I say I "know" Ohio State University, I mean that my knowledge is direct and first-hand. The player knows baseball or golf or football; the spectator knows about it.

In advocating immediate knowledge, I do not decry mediated knowledge or knowledge about. Far from it. But we must not take leave of our senses and neglect warm, compelling, and sometimes poignant first-hand experiences.

This is the stuff out of which mature concepts are developed. We must realize that there is a continuing interaction between the concrete and the abstract; the greater the depth of the concrete experience, the greater the height of the abstraction.

We need a heightened awareness of the world around us, its sounds, sights, odors, and colors. We must sense it. This sensitivity, this awareness, will enable us to listen with the "third ear," the ear of compassion. It brings into sharper focus what we were only dimly aware of, and we see unexpected likenesses and differences.

Here we enlist the help of the writer, the painter, the musician, the poet, and the creator in all media who keeps saying: look and listen to what you never really saw or heard before. We develop artistic concerns. We see the new in the old, the old in the new. Clearly, then, our curriculum must not neglect the attitudes and emotional life of the learner. Pascal once said, "The heart has reasons which the reason knows not of." And the Irish poet James Stephens said, "The heart will understand today what the mind understands tomorrow."

Indeed, our stress on the cognitive goals of education

must always be matched with a similar stress on the affective, the emotional, and the attitudinal. Here lies the driving source of power. The mind illuminates the way, and the heart helps us push ahead on our journey.

That knowledge is of most worth that enables persons and societies to know where it hurts, and know what to do not only to relieve the pain, but also to cure it. Many now try to relieve their pain by thoughtless nonconformity which may turn out to be simply conformity to another point of view.

Great art can break down the walls that many of us erect against painful or sorrowful experiences. We are likely to think that what we do not know will not hurt us, but it is this capacity for being hurt that distinguishes the sensitive man from the insensitive one.

That knowledge is of most worth which enhances the mutuality of human beings and develops a sense of community, the doing of important things together. The words "synergy" and "symbiosis" are helpful at this point. Why can't we have students teach each other? Students now do this informally in preparing for examinations. Why not make it a regular part of the instructional program of the school? We have all discovered that we learn something well when we try to teach it to someone else. Further, why do we assume that we must bring in outside resource persons. We fail to realize that the rich experiences of students are first-hand, easily available resources of learning?

That knowledge is of most worth which enables an individual to see the cause-and-effect relationships between his choices and their consequences, a characteristic of a moral man. Besides asking what happened, people need to ask why it happened, what will happen next, and what difference, if any, that it makes. People need to consider the secondary as well as the primary consequences of their choices. For example, when we decrease the early deaths of small children and lengthen the lives of the elderly, we must face the primary and secondary effects of a population increase. In other words, the knowledge of most worth is that which enables people to be foresighted in their thinking, to predict the consequences of their choices, and, when necessary, to change their course of action.

That knowledge is of most worth which helps individuals recognize knowledge that is of most worth. This means learning to judge values, and to recognize the difference between the permanent and the ephemeral, the important and the trivial, and the rational and the irrational. What we consider valuable should be based on an examination and comparison of values.

In a world brimming with new knowledge it is not enough to ask whether learning has worth. We must ask rather: what learning is of *most* worth? That knowledge is of most worth which enhances the dignity of persons. To dignify man is to honor, to exalt, to make worthy. It is easy to say this, but to translate it into reality is today's great challenge.

CHAPTER V

Learning to Learn

In our schools and colleges we try to cram enough learning into the first third of life to last the next two-thirds. We do not directly prepare our students for continuing lifelong education; we prepare them for graduation from high school and college. In an unpredictable world, all of us must learn to learn and to develop a taste for learning. Indeed, the chief product of learning may well be the process of learning.

Every learner must develop the motivation to learn—the *want-to*—and he must couple this with the methods and the materials of learning—the *know-how* and the *know-why*. Therefore, his curriculum will be not only the subject matter of a field but the associated learning process as well. He must, in short, consciously learn how to process information, ideas, and subject matter.

Characteristics of Learning to Learn
Every learner must learn how to get his ignorance organized and how to judge what knowledge is of most worth. Students must learn not only to distinguish the poor from the good, but the better from the best. They must realize that day by day, consciously or unconsciously, they are choosing their standards. A sloppy presentation,

a carelessly written theme, or allowing "good enough" to be a substitute for "good" are all results of inefficient, inept, and thoughtless learning. The excellence that is demanded by high standards is needed in auto repair just as it is needed in nursing or surgery.

Students must learn to see subtle differences in books and magazines, in drama and films, in poetry, and in personal conduct, where previously they saw either gross differences or no differences at all. They must discern these differences themselves, not merely memorize what other discriminating persons have seen. Learning is like eating or sleeping. A person must do it himself; it can't be delegated.

Too much school and college learning is shallow. If we learn to attack problems in depth, our usable memory of that subject will be greater, and our ability to learn from it will be enhanced. Further, the enjoyment that comes from really knowing a subject will make it unnecessary to have someone around to keep winding us up. Instead, we can become self-winding and self-sustaining in our intellectual activities. Success in learning will provide increasingly strong motivation. Indeed, the best motivation for success is success itself.

In mastering any subject, in learning to learn, we must map the field, note its basic principles, its key ideas and vocabulary, and its conceptual structure. For example, no sensible person studies the automobile by first trying to master the names of all its parts. Instead, he thinks in terms of systems—ignition, fuel, transmission, braking, and so on. In each of these classes there are meaningfully related concepts, for example, spark plug, condenser, timer, and carburetor. The basic vocabulary must be learned.

The solution of problems requires that we quickly bring dissimilar ideas together, a process that requires one's mental scanning system to operate at full efficiency. The crux of learning is to develop a conceptual scheme for skillful filing of experience. This means constant practice in school and college on the filing and retrieval of past experiences, and a shift from asking only: what did the textbook or reference volume say? to: what ideas do I already have that I can bring to bear upon solving this problem?

A person who is learning to learn searches for relationships—for the ways by which he can put experiences together more meaningfully. Let us apply this to concept development. Nearly every college student has come into contact with such words as "dystrophy," "eugenic," "dyspeptic," "euphoria," or "euthanasia." If he has learned a method of word attack which emphasizes meaningful similarities and differences in roots, suffixes, and prefixes, he will note here the use of two prefixes, *eu* and *dys*. He discovers that they apparently mean good and bad.

He will now test out his hypothesis. If "eulogy" means "good words," is there then a word "dyslogy" which means "bad words"? There is such a word. One might experiment further and create such words as "dysphoria," "dysgenic," and "eupeptic." When he meets the word "eudemonic," he can check the context to see if it means "good demon." It is a little hard to work "eudemonic" into a dinner table conversation, but we ought to learn some things just for our own amazement.

Many persons know such words as "neuritis," "anemia," "claustrophobia," and "psychosis." But many have not learned through discovery the following root meanings: *itis*-inflammation; *emia*-blood; *phobia*-fear; and *osis*-diseased or abnormal condition. Many persons deny ever having seen a trigon but know what a pentagon is. Few graduate students have learned that *gon* means angle, as in "agonic," "bigonial," "nonagon," or, indeed, "trigonometry."

In learning to learn it is often helpful to build outlines, models, and paradigms as a way of classifying ideas. Thus one develops a ready system for filing, reclassifying, and retrieving past experience. I have found it useful to think about the communication process in terms of the following outline:

Producing Messages   Consuming Messages

	Reading	Listening	Observing
Writing	✓		
Speaking (including music)		✓	
Visualizing (including plastic arts)			✓

It shows visually that communication involves both the producing and consuming of ideas and that three pairs of associated abilities are needed: reading-writing, listening-speaking, and observing-visualizing. One can also see that, as the cells are filled in, there are many other possible combinations, for example, reading and listening, and visualizing and listening.

The typical curriculum in English or reading now emphasizes reading-writing and speaking-listening, but rarely deals in depth with visualizing-observing as one of the key phases of communication. Thus many teachers ignore the pervasive, mediated experiences of television, motion pictures, and photographs—major aspects of the communication process. They may also ignore the creating of drama experience with the plastic arts, producing paintings, or making films.

What all learners need, then, is a well-organized, effective way to get in touch with the best ideas in the world. We might do this by listening and discussion, as did the early Greeks or the early Christians. We may learn by observing what others have visualized in paintings, drawings, photographs, motion pictures, or television.

These language skills and abilities are closely alike in some ways and have many transferable elements, and yet some sharp differences. Listening and speaking, for example, are "mastered" before reading and writing, because they are closer to reality. Written words have been described as symbols of symbols.

We usually speak more simply than we read or write. It is in speaking and in listening that our patterns of language are established. Here is where the warmly emotional is communicated, the subtle nuances of feeling which are not so easily conveyed in writing and reading. It is in speaking and listening, too, that we are still struggling awkwardly to share ideas in formal or informal discussions. There always seems to be more speakers than listeners. Disciplined speaking and listening are necessary in learning how to learn.

Many of our how-to-learn skills deal with specialized ways of reading and reporting. Has the typical junior high school student mastered the basic skills required to use reference materials? Does he understand a card catalog system? Can he quickly find what he is looking for in a dictionary? Does he understand the pronunciation guide? Does he know the meaning of the various mathematical symbols? One study showed that only 10 percent of the freshmen in a large university knew how to use a library.

What aspect of learning to learn is involved in observing and viewing? We must remember that high school students spend about as much time looking at television as they do in school. Have we taught them the art of skillful, critical viewing? If they do not master the mass media, the mass media will master them. They will be overwhelmed with triviality and carried away by temporary excitement about things that do not really matter. Instead, their critical ability should grow year by year. How does the seventh grader differ from the ninth grader in his ability to evaluate critically a news program or a dramatic program on television? If there are no differences, why aren't there? The ability to learn how to learn should improve throughout life.

The educated man has learned to observe people, things, and events. He has learned to observe directly as well as to learn from books and from conversation. He has mastered the habit of sizing up a situation, diagnosing it, and then planning what to do about it. We say: when you have a tough job to do, give it to a busy man. This is not because his efficient secretary may do much of the work; it is chiefly because he has learned the art of getting things done efficiently and effectively. He has learned how to learn.

The person who has learned how to learn has these characteristics:

(1) A heightened sensitivity to things that matter
(2) A feeling of continuing and cumulative power and growth in understanding
(3) The delight that comes from discovery
(4) An effective system for finding, mentally filing, and retrieving ideas
(5) Flexibility in transferring ideas from one situation to another
(6) Ease in obtaining meaning from words and images
(7) A zest for more learning.

A person who is moving toward maturity in reaching these goals has learned to be independent. He is developing a wide-ranging critical mind of his own. The disciplined mind will not be easily achieved through mere attendance at school or college; it must be actively and rigorously sought as a major goal of all education.

The thinking person has learned how to learn. He is not time-bound or space-bound. He is not provincial in his outlook, nor is he a willing slave to the comfortable routines of the present. He will find his way in a troubled and complicated world, whether the date is 1971 or 2001.

Principles of Learning

I have presented some of the characteristics of the art and science of learning how to learn. Let us now look more closely at the concept of learning and ask what the psychologists say about the factors involved in successful learning. The application of these principles to our learning or to teaching should increase the productivity of both students and learners. Clearly, materials and methods of instruction should reflect the use of these principles and thereby help students learn more, learn it faster, remember it better, and apply it more skillfully.

The generalizations about learning noted below have helped me as a teacher and as a learner. Even if criticized as being only common sense, the indictment is not severe.

(1) *The clearer and the more realistic and relevant the statement of desired outcomes, the more effective the learning.* If you cannot see the target clearly, the chances of hitting it are not good. The experimental psychologist Samuel Renshaw says, "Be sure the learner knows what is expected of him from the first."

Many teachers do not work from a carefully planned course and unit outline in which the desired goals are carefully differentiated into information, intellectual processes, skills, and values. Nor is there typically a systematic plan for teaching these objectives that uses all effective media of communication, including programmed instruction. Educational goals are not usually simply and clearly presented; they tend to be fancy, diffuse, and woolly, and expanded beyond what can be accomplished.

(2) *We learn what we practice.* The most commonly practiced skill in school and college is memorizing for temporary learning, and many students are highly proficient at it. The movement for accountability for learning outcomes is likely to sharpen objectives and to commit them more strongly to permanent learning. You cannot be accountable unless you know what your learning goals are and regularly practice the required skills.

As we study typical course outlines, we see that learning by discovery, critical reading, and discriminating judgment—the thinking processes—are commonly stated as objectives. However, we cannot learn to think or read critically without guided practice. Further, mere practice does not make perfect. You can practice error as well as accuracy. Neither does repetition ensure learning; indeed, it may cause boredom and distaste. Renshaw says, "Repetition does not produce learning, but merely presents sufficient opportunities for the reorganization of the process through approximation and correction."

Effective practice requires a model to be imitated. Does the classroom instruction provide models of persons skillfully thinking, painting, writing, composing, or solving problems? What provisions are there for practicing excellence? How good is the coaching? As you proceeded through elementary school, high school, and college, did you have excellent models to imitate? If you are a teacher, do you now provide these desirable models?

If we learn what we practice, then we should practice in the way we wish finally to perform. Sloppy practice means sloppy learning. You cannot practice mediocrity and come out with excellence. We permit students to practice learning in a style and tempo that is less than their best. Poor, inefficient practice may be worse than no practice at all; it is concentrated, thoughtful, regular, and spaced practice that educates.

(3) You must teach for transfer. Previous learning does not automatically transfer to new learning. For example, the professor of chemistry concerned about advancing knowledge by research in his own field may not transfer this research interest to his own teaching methods.

All of us have a large reservoir of inert knowledge, which does not help us solve new problems because we have not practiced ways of transferring this knowledge to new situations. We need guided practice in learning to transform or reconstruct our habitual way of doing things.

We can increase transfer by practicing our new learning in varied contexts, by noting many illustrations of a generalization in addition to those in the textbook. Most students, when asked to give an example of algae will usually mention algae growing in ponds. If a newly learned term or principle is to be widely transferred and become enriched with association, many applications must be noted and practiced. We use it often or we lose it.

We can increase transfer by generalizing or intellectualizing our experiences, by developing concepts, and by searching for an emerging principle. The habit of seeing relationships and unity in apparent diversity can be widely transferred. Learning by discovery gives practice in building insight.

We can increase transfer by building attitudes favorable to learning. How often do students take a course in which they are actively encouraged to become curious and concerned? Sometimes transfer is negative, and we learn to dislike a subject, a tremendous loss of productivity. A junior high school student of mine at Winnetka, Ill., asked his Latin teacher at New Trier High School why the study of Latin was important. He did not get an answer; instead, he was scolded for being impertinent. This was a simple and quick way for the instructor to kill interest in Latin.

Transfer may be thwarted by premature verbalization. We may *talk* too much before we act. Some overt or intuitive doing is probably a necessary condition for fruitful verbalization of principles. Dewey says, "An ounce of experience is better than a ton of theory, simply because it is only as an experience that any theory has vital and verifiable significance. . . . A theory apart from an experience cannot be definitely grasped even as a theory."

(4) Learning is increased by knowledge of results. If correct responses are to be rewarded, the learner must get prompt, reenforcing feedback. The beginning golfer who made a hole in one asked his instructor, "What did I do right?" Learning behavior must be diagnosed and remedial measures proposed when necessary. Delayed approval or disapproval is not highly motivating.

The nature of the feedback depends on the objectives of instruction. If we edit a student's paper for "mechanical" errors and do not give him feedback on the logic and quality of ideas expressed, he may learn to be mechanically correct but illogical. Or he may learn to dislike writing. Lou LaBrant asks in *We Teach English*, "Will your comments lead [the student] to write again, or to fear writing? Will you stimulate a desire to write better, or merely a fear of making errors?"

(5) There is a motivation factor in all learning. Nothing motivates like success. We learn when we are rewarded and fail to learn when we are punished. Although what is rewarding to one student may not be rewarding to another, teacher enthusiasm and peer group acceptance are generally important factors in motivation.

Immediate rewards usually produce more learning than delayed rewards, and intrinsic rewards are better than extrinsic ones. We can learn to be motivated by both present and future rewards. Immature persons must have all their rewards right now, but the mature person has learned that the future as well as the present can be rewarding.

Praise is better than scolding. Do we praise good ideas or only the absence of errors? Are we stingy with pats on the back and generous with slaps on the wrists? We need systematic plans for commending satisfying performance, and we need equally a supporting climate of learning. James Coleman said in his report, *Equality & Educational Opportunity,* that "Of all the variables measured in the survey, the attitudes of student interest in school, self-concept and sense of environmental control show the strongest relation to achievement."

If success is the best motivation for learning, then we must artfully arrange sequences of instruction for maximal success. And we must help students learn to arrange their own sequences. Perhaps, too, a "cafeteria" of learning materials will enable students to select experiences in which they can secure daily success.

We must not be beguiled by the notion that learning is a series of simple little steps, taken without reference to a broad pattern and without reference to preceding material or material to follow. A well-developed programmed curriculum has been sequenced for the most productive learning. Sometimes we will have to do it on a step-by-step basis, especially when some of the steps are critical. But the most important programming for learning is self-programming, what we eventually do for ourselves.

(6) We learn best what is meaningful. No one would advocate meaninglessness in education, but every day teachers and texts present unclear materials to students. Rote methods of teaching and learning are common.

A typical remedy when students do not understand is "more of the same"—work harder and read the materials over and over again. Some suggest that the frustration and challenge of difficult materials are a necessary part of learning. This may sometimes be true, but there are plenty of genuine barriers to learning without inventing additional ones. We climb mountains because they are there, but we do not climb them for the same reason.

Since students learn best by varying methods, we must, therefore, use varied experiences in teaching. The most meaningful experiences provide a means to our own goals. Hadley Cantril said "No occurrence is an event for us until it has some bearing on our purposes."

(7) Most people never reach their potential. The data from measurement of mental ability and achievement are sometimes accepted as defining the upper limits of student potential. We also use these data to sort out or classify students and to explain failures on the basis of low test scores. But such data are not adequate predictors of college success. Further, low correlation between mental ability tests and creativity is not uncommon.

A major development in the future will be the discovery of undeveloped talent. For this purpose, sensitive diagnostic instruments are necessary; it is also necessary to develop educational programs based on such a diagnosis.

Let us assume, for example, that the tests disclosed potential dramatic talent. What could a person do about this today? There are few public and repertory theaters. We must, therefore, assess our communities with the aim of providing fertile soil for the flowering of all kinds of talent. Our present counseling tools are too blunt and insensitive.

Given high motivation and superior teaching, notable

changes can be made in student learning. This is well-illustrated in sports, where all the modern media of instruction are used to develop the potential of promising football players. These include specialized coaching, special meals, and film analysis of performance combined with extensive public praise.

Some happy day we may spend as much money developing excellent readers and writers as we now spend to develop superb athletes. When that time comes, we shall discover many late bloomers, a rich abundance of undeveloped talent.

I have stated repeatedly in this book that the environment or the atmosphere in which we learn is critically important. Learning blossoms in a mood of mutuality. Too often the professor is more interested in his subject than he is in his student. This is not too bad for highly motivated persons at the graduate level or even at the undergraduate level, but even the brightest and ablest students in college take to their hearts the professor who sees them as persons and not as positions on a seat chart.

We must be careful, therefore, lest the school or college atmosphere be too formal, too formidable, or too schoolteacherish. Learning, after all, does not look like a textbook; it surrounds you and becomes incorporated into your life.

CHAPTER VI

Thinking About Thinking

Most of us would be pleased to be described as a person who thinks for himself. Critical thinking is an educational goal as desirable as good health. Former Harvard president Nathan M. Pusey has said that the job of the university is "to educate free, independent, and vigorous minds, capable of analyzing events, of exercising judgment, of distinguishing facts from propaganda and truth from half-truth and lies." He is talking about critical thinking, a central task of the school from kindergarten through graduate school.

Critical thinking is thinking which has been systematically criticized. It criticizes not only the means used to reach goals but the goals themselves; it evaluates our values. It is meeting a fork-in-the-road situation for which no neat, exact map already exists. It is the kind of sustained thinking necessary to deal adequately with such questions as: How can we develop an equitable taxing system? What safeguards does modern technology require? What is worth waiting for?

Sometimes the critical issue faced by an individual is that of defining the question. Obviously, we cannot find the answer until we are clear about the question; we must both define and confine the problem. A friend of inventor Charles Kettering had the idea of teaching people to think by using jigsaw puzzles. Kettering pointed out, however, that in a jigsaw puzzle the limits of the problem have already been defined; one only puts the available pieces together. Life, he said, is like a jigsaw puzzle in which you do not know the outer dimensions of the puzzle, and sometimes you do not have all the pieces.

Do schools and colleges help students get ready to solve important problems and learn how to criticize thinking? Paul Dressel's and Lewis Mayhew's study, *General Education: Explorations in Evaluations*, of college teaching in nineteen universities and colleges is not encouraging. Their committee on social sciences found that:

> . . . little was being done to teach for critical thinking. . . . Attempts to teach critical thinking in social science by making minor changes in particular courses did not appear to result in greater growth than was found in courses not making overt attempts to teach this skill. . . . Observations of classes and interviews with students suggest that students in typical humanities courses read assignments from textbooks, and then come to class either to listen passively to a teacher tell them *about* some work of art or to listen to or see a work about which they have studied. . . . If the objectives of increased participation, analytical ability or genuine appreciation are valid, then the way many humanities courses are conducted must be judged inadequate.

The teaching of critical thinking in the social sciences, Dressel and Mayhew have noted, should produce the ability to (1) identify central issues, (2) recognize underlying assumptions, (3) evaluate evidence or authority, and (4) draw warranted conclusions. Item (3), "to evaluate evidence or authority," is subdivided into the ability to recognize stereotypes and clichés, recognize bias and emotional factors in a presentation, distinguish between relevant and nonrelevant, distinguish between essential and incidental, recognize the adequacy of data, determine whether facts support a generalization, and check consistency.

Admittedly, the thinking abilities noted here are not simple or easily achieved. Nevertheless, they have simple beginnings, which can be undertaken in the elementary and high school and the college. Who is doing the thinking in the schools and colleges? Is it the students? The teachers? Both? The critical decision we must make as teachers or administrators is whether we want the school to train or to educate. The issue is one directly related to critical thinking as a goal.

Critical Thinking in Reading, Listening, and Observing

The thoughtful reader, listener, or observer (as contrasted with the trained one) will not passively accept what is read, heard, or seen. Similar thoughtfulness is required in writing, speaking, and visualizing. Although the following discussion emphasizes reading, the principles also apply to listening and observing.

Reading can be roughly organized into three levels of thinking. The first level is simple, uncritical reproduction, a duplication of what has been read. This requires thinking, of course, but the skills are readily predictable. It is *reading the lines*—merely viewing a photograph or exhibit. It is literal comprehension. The reader knows what the author "said," no small accomplishment. What did he mean?

The second and higher level of thinking involves drawing inferences and discovering the implications. To interpret cartoons, for example, we must *read between the lines*. It requires critical thinking, an analysis of what the message really meant, and the use of the higher mental processes. Did the author write ironically with tongue in cheek? Was his tone helpful? cynical? an exaggeration for effect?

A third level of thinking involves interpretation, evaluation, and application of what is read, heard, or seen and requires vigorous, critical judgment. It is *reading beyond the lines.* One must "distinguish facts from propaganda and truth from half-truth and lies", as noted above by Pusey. Hence we have three levels of thinking: duplication, implication, and application.

We will deal more specifically with some characteristics of critical reading and offer suggestions for developing the critical reader. These points also apply directly to critical listening and observing.

(1) *Critical reading is independent reading.* It is independent in the sense that thinking—like loving or appreciating—is an individual, personal affair, not initially a group process. The critical reader is often on his own—self-directed, not teacher-directed. He is becoming an independent learner, one who has learned how to learn, and loves learning.

(2) *Critical reading is problem centered.* One of the key tasks of critical reading is to find and state the problem, the key issue. If you cannot identify the problem, you cannot solve it. Further, without critical analysis we are likely to treat symptoms, not causes.

(3) *Critical reading is analytical and judgmental.* A literary critic analyzes a book and then passes judgment on it, noting its strengths and weaknesses. He probes hidden assumptions and evaluates the logic or illogic of the writer. He must present his best judgments, demonstrate his awareness of critical standards, and indicate either directly or inferentially, whether this book is worth reading. Critical reading is disciplined reading by persons who have convictions about something.

(4) *Critical reading is based on a stubborn effort to get at the truth.* The critical reader must be aware of all the barriers to the truth, many of them in his own mind. He must learn that we see the world through the lenses of our own experience. Perceptions are personal: the eye sees

what it knows. Even eminent scientists may be bumbling amateurs when they try to think outside the field of their competency.

If a critical-minded student in a high school history class asks, "How do we know whether an event occurred the way the author described it?" he is facing the question of historical evidence. How does a good historian behave when he deals with an event in which he is personally involved? Lord Acton instructed the contributors to the *Cambridge Modern History* to write as if situated "in Long. 30 degrees W." in the middle of the Atlantic Ocean. The critical thinker, like the historian, must make a conscious and disciplined effort to get at the truth. He persistently asks: what is the evidence?

Obviously, the disciplined chronicler of history must bring logical thinking to bear in collecting evidence. But is logical thinking enough? Does it meet all the needs of critical and creative thinking? Do our neat and supposedly logical arrangements for teaching subject matter always fit the varied outcomes which we are seeking? Is it true, as Harold Lasswell notes in *Psychopathology and Politics*, that "The ultimate paradox of logical thinking is that it is self-destroying when it is too sedulously cultivated. . . . It becomes intolerant of the immediate, unanalyzed, primitive abundance of the mind, and by so doing destroys its own source."

(5) *Critical reading is creative, imaginative, and nonconformist.* Here we can contrast training and education. Reading can be taught as training—with fixed limits and predictable responses. Genuinely educational experiences, however, have no ceiling, no fixed boundaries, and no neat terminal points. Critical reading, like critical listening and observing, is a creative, imaginative, reflective interaction with a writer, a speaker, or a visualizer. Life is a jigsaw puzzle without neat limits and with pieces missing, as inventor Kettering noted, and therefore demands critical thinking.

(6) *The critical reader associates with the best minds of all generations.* One of the best ways to do this is to read thoughtfully, analytically, judgmentally, and critically. Ezra Pound once said, "Literature is news that stays news." Certainly the wisdom of Shakespeare has remained news for four hundred years, and the insight of Cervantes, Boswell, and Thoreau have present day applications. The best minds of all generations have been creating beautiful sounds and rich and evocative images.

(7) *Critical reading is an involving, participatory experience.* Walt Whitman once said, "Books are to be called for and supplied, on the assumption that the process of reading is not a half sleep, but in the highest sense, an exercise, a gymnast's struggle; that the reader is to do something for himself." The unthinking passivity of routine acceptance is a great hazard in listening and observing as well.

The word "dialogue" has been overused, but it does have rich meaning. In critical evaluation you have a dialogue, a conversation with the "author." You ask him tough questions, and sometimes you feel that he answers them well, and sometimes that he answers badly. The critical thinker will ask the age-old questions that everyone faces and tries to answer: Who am I? What am I here for? What is worth doing? How responsible am I for my neighbor, and who is my neighbor? What really makes a difference?

(8) *The critical reader is sensitive to words and has acquired an excellent vocabulary.* To read and think critically we must savor the flavor of words and make subtle discriminations among meanings of words—for example, "irony," "sarcasm," and "satire," or "burlesque" and "farce." The critical reader must be able to spell lest he confuse "perimeter" with "parameter," "council" with "counsel," "broach" with "brooch," or "arraign" with "arrange". The critical reader is sensitive to metaphor, a way of making words do extra work. He is at home with

terms like "synecdoche," "oxymoron," "metonymy," and "litotes."

Meager vocabularies betray our failure to read widely and critically. For example, a young woman reportedly approached Robert Hutchins after a lecture and said, "You were simply superfluous. I've never heard such an enervating speech."

"Thank you," Hutchins replied. "I'm thinking of having it published posthumously."

"Wonderful," replied the young woman, "and the sooner the better."

(9) *The critical reader reads to remember, not to forget.* What the thinking reader selects to read should not only be worth remembering but also worth reflecting on and talking about. Knowledge unshared is knowledge forgotten. Critical reading, listening, and observing are active, not passive, mental processes. The uncritical reader often reads to erase experience, but the critical reader tries to make a mentally indelible record of what he has read.

Thinking as Choosing

All education involves the development and refinement of choice—an awareness of alternatives and the need to study and mentally rehearse the possible consequences of these alternatives before choosing them. To choose wisely is to live well, and the story of every man's life lies in the quality of big and little choices, the options that he selects.

In *Can People Learn to Learn?* psychiatrist Brock Chisholm says:

> The sort of questions an active, free, and well-developed imagination will answer truly are, "What will happen if I do so and so?" "What will be the result if I go to such and such a place?" "What will be the effect if I say this or that?" "Will those happenings, results, or effects be desirable for me? For others? For my relationship with myself and with others?" "Will they enhance or outweigh and

diminish whatever satisfactions I may expect my actions to produce?"

What will happen if . . .? Here the experience of the individual becomes critical. We all operate in the present, but we can either merely exist in a restricted, narrow present, or we can act in an amplified present, a present illuminated by our past experiences and our thoughtful hopes for the future. For some, this circle of illumination has a wide diameter; for others this circle is limited.

We all make some poor choices, the consequence of living in a world where there are many options. If we make poor choices, we ask: Where and how did my thinking go wrong? Did I operate with the best information I could get, or did I choose hastily and carelessly? The mature person has learned that he is responsible for his own choices, hence the importance in an educative environment of helping people become aware that they are choosing—by default sometimes, but choosing nevertheless.

The role of the teacher in the thinking process is to give just enough help but not too much. To give too much help is to reward dependency, and to rob the student of the joy and risks of independent thinking. To give too little needed guidance is to frustrate the learner.

The teacher's task, then, in developing insightful choice making is to be chiefly a guide and coach. His major task is not to provide the basic information on which excellent choices are made, but rather to stimulate the student to think independently about choices and their consequences, and also to develop values. The student must learn to find his own information and become his own programmer of learning. Obviously, the teacher and the librarian will assist him in finding relevant materials and choosing from among available learning resources.

Thinking as Discovery

More than three hundred years ago Comenius wrote that his object was "to seek and find a *method* by which teachers teach less and learners learn more." In 1860

Herbert Spencer wrote as follows in *Education: Intellectual, Moral and Physical:*

> Children should be led to make their own investigations, and to draw their own inferences. They should be told as little as possible, and induced to *discover* as much as possible. Humanity has progressed solely by self-instruction; and . . . to achieve the best results, each mind must progress somewhat after the same fashion.

Interest in learning by discovery in several school subjects has increased sharply. Publications of the National Council of Teachers of Mathematics have emphasized that "all students should repeatedly and continuously be 'led' to discover or 'invent' mathematical concepts and ideas for themselves." Suggestions on how to reach this objective are found in "Telling Methods versus Heuristic Methods" in N. L. Gage's *Handbook of Research on Teaching.*

The need for students to discover patterns in solving arithmetic problems has been a long-time concern of researcher Guy T. Buswell. Data from his study, *Patterns of Thinking in Solving Problems,* showed that schools were not achieving any marked success in reaching this objective. "Rather the thinking of the . . . subjects indicates an absence of a generalized mode of problem solving." He also noted "the need for increased ability to read problems. . . . The basic difficulty was failure to *read critically* [my emphasis] in order to separate relevant and irrelevant facts." Buswell recommends that teachers shift their major concern from the answers obtained to the methods of thinking by which answers are obtained. In reading unfamiliar material, the student is asked to infer the meaning of hard words by noting their context.

But unless a student has a structure or pattern with which to work, he cannot systematically make disciplined guesses, inferences, and conclusions. When his subject matter is organic (organized), it means that a system of relationships has been established. These, in turn, create new relationships. Most subjects as now taught do not generate either the discovery of principles or critical thinking.

Discovery is of two kinds—what we are looking for directly and what we may not be looking for at all. Serendipity will produce an unexpected bonus, something gained not by a direct search but as an outcome of a direct search for something else. We are, however, most likely to discover something if we are searching for an answer to a well-formulated question.

We can also learn more than one thing at a time through concomitant or secondary learning. We can aim to discover the *why* and *how* of experience as we are learning the *what*. Furthermore, all learning can develop a vigorous spirit of inquiry, new ways of doing things, and improved effeciency. A taste for learning can grow and develop.

How much should the teacher tell the student and what should the student discover for himself? Further, what are the powers of self-discovery among students? Who can make what kinds of inferential leaps? How many need the small steps of some programmed instruction? How many can take giant steps?

These are difficult questions to answer. But no matter what the final answer may be, *we should give all students the opportunity to test their powers to make judgments and to draw inferences*. They must be faced with problems, puzzles, dilemmas, and issues which cause them to "rack their brains;" too often, they begin to read instead of to think.

Perhaps they already have the data with which to solve the problem. In fact, many students are told answers to questions which they could figure out for themselves. But this takes time and we are organized for telling and reciting, not for thinking. For example, most persons do not know the date of the Gettysburg Address, yet they could figure it out if they knew and understood the first line: "Fourscore and seven years ago our fathers brought forth on this continent a new nation. . . ." To figure out the date they must know the meaning of the word "score" (it is 20 not 10, as many students believe) and when our country was founded. So they now add 87 and 1776 and discover the date to be 1863.

Why is there not more learning by discovery? William James noted that most of us become enslaved to stock conceptions: "Genius, in truth, means little more than the faculty of perceiving in an unhabitual way." But how do we learn to see the world in unhabitual ways? One approach is to recognize and list underlying assumptions of our various educational institutions. The school, for example, assumes that children should go to school five days a week for forty weeks. Why not four or six days a week for forty-eight weeks, a year-round school? We usually have about thirty children in a self-contained classroom. Why not thirty-five, with additional specialists or assistants paid out of the money saved by increasing class size? Why not teach five children at one time in a math center in fourth grade?

In high school or college, students study four or five major subjects. Why not three? Or six? What would happen if students in certain subjects rarely met in regular classes at all, but worked on specially prepared study materials? The chances are good that with able coaching they would learn a great deal. What group learning could be changed to individual instruction? And conversely, what individual instruction might be done better in a group? Must we have twelve years of elementary and secondary instruction? Why not reduce it by one year? The University of Michigan is now experimenting with a five-year medical curriculum.

We have seen that learning by discovery is a search for new meanings, for developing transferable generalizations drawn from concrete experiences. We abstract these experiences from their specific concepts and generalize them, often in verbal form. Some writers have pointed out, however, that there is danger in premature abstractions, in verbalizing too soon. Further, we can successfully generalize without verbalizing; artists do this all the time.

We face, then, the twin hazards of getting stuck in the concrete or lost in the misty clouds of abstraction.

Creativity and the Thinking Process

In today's world, creativity is not just a nice thing to have; it is a grave necessity. We need more innovation and invention, first, to save the world from self-destruction, and second, to contribute to the mental health and power of individuals. Imitating the past is not good enough; only the creative society will survive.

In teaching and learning, therefore, we face a choice between imitative reaction and creative interaction. Since our schools and colleges emphasize chiefly imitative reaction, the resulting learning by rote will be inadequate for future needs.

Suppose we want to promote creativity in several fields of study. How do we go about it? For example, how do you read creatively? Many students believe that the best way to master an assignment is to read it over and over again. But is it? The best evidence is that rethinking a passage is often more productive in terms of time spent than rereading it. The students who recreate rather than reread are reorganizing the material and putting it into their own filing systems, readily available for later use.

Can you teach a person to be a creative writer, obviously a person who can think critically? John Ciardi said in the *Saturday Review* (Dec. 15, 1956):

> The truly creative—whether in art, in science, or in philosophy—is always and precisely that which cannot be taught And yet, though it seems paradoxical, creativity cannot spring from the untaught. Creativity is the imaginatively gifted recombination of old elements into new. And so, it may be seen that there is no real paradox. The elements of an invention or of a creation can be taught; but the creativity must be self-discovered and self-disciplined.

What about creativity in personal relationships? Does it, like creative writing, involve "the imaginatively gifted recombination of old elements into new"? We envy but do not always imitate those persons who are unusually creative in the art of being friendly. They exhibit those heartwarming nuances of taste and conduct which distinguish a gracious person from an ordinary one. We all remember with appreciation those insightful comments that creative teachers with extrasensitive perception wrote on our papers. The instructor saw us as a person and cared about what we said.

We need to take a fresh, inventive look at the curricula of schools and colleges. It is clear that they are geared to "input" but not to "output." We spend too much time acquiring information (often for temporary purposes) and too little time in creative processing and reorganizing, and in putting information to work. We are more concerned about reproducing knowledge than we are about producing it. We emphasize the duplication of knowledge but do too little with creative explication, implication, and application. We need more "learning *for* doing."

Let us suppose that we tried to set up a school environment highly conducive to creative thinking and learning. What would it be like?

It would be one which embodied great respect for the dignity and the importance of every student. There would be a higher level of self-discipline, of dedication, and of personal responsibility for learning. Openness to experience would be considered a critical goal of the curriculum. We would cherish the opening of minds and shun the closing of minds. We would try to unfreeze "frozen perceptions."

We would look for administrators and supervisors who consider creativity a critical and important goal of the school, and, indeed, select them for *their* creativity. In the creative school we will be less concerned about the excessively smooth conformist and have greater concern for the slightly elliptical, occasionally abrasive personality.

We would sharply increase the quality and variety of instructional materials, and provide more nonverbal learning for its own sake and as a preparation for verbal learning. Our teaching materials today require high verbal proficiency, yet the creative persons are not necessarily the fluent verbalists. We may be neglecting potential painters, photographers, musicians, and architects by failing to see the role of nonverbal experience.

Can we press too hard for a creative approach to all problems? Certainly we do not want creative spelling. How much change can we stand without future shock? We should aim for an appropriate balance between creative flexibility and the stability provided by current knowledge. We should be aware, too, that some people cannot live comfortably with tentativeness or tolerate ambiguity; they need a large amount of structure.

To be creative is to be thoughtfully involved, to be a concerned and active participant, not a disengaged spectator. Creativity is an experience in depth which transforms pleasure into joy, entertainment into delight, and listless apathy into dynamic living.

The Liberated Mind

If we want to live in the "land of the free and the home of the brave," it will take rigorous thinking to do it. To be free is to be in charge of one's own life, to be conscious of one's developing powers, and to be open to new ideas, not closed to them. It is to be skilled in understanding causes and effects, and to become increasingly adept in forecasting the consequences of our actions. It is to learn day by day that everything is related. To be free is to prize diversity and pluralism, and to oppose prejudice, totalitarianism, and fanaticism.

Finally, there are few satisfactions greater than being your own man, living a thoughtful life where few hostages have been given to fortune, and achieving your own unique values. What, then, do many people, young and old, really want? They want more uncluttered space, physically and spiritually. They want a place where they can sit down without having someone tell them to move over. They want more people to practice what Rudyard Kipling called "the art of judicious letting alone."

They want a socially productive economy instead of mindless waste; they want their money's worth, whatever they buy. They want to spend their life for something that will outlast it, as William James put it. They want people around them who are worth imitating. If we wish to develop thoughtfully creative individuals, then we must value them enough to do something to increase their number. We must place this goal high on our personal and national agenda, and think harder about thinking.

CHAPTER VII

Process and Product

The terms "process" and "product" deserve special attention as we consider instructional methods and materials. In educational discussion today process is often emphasized rather than product, form rather than content. It is beguiling to see life as flowing, growing, dynamic, rather than unchanging and static. John Dewey became interested in Newtonian calculus and especially liked the word "fluxion" because it "treats of flowing numbers." Fluxion is the rate of change of a continuously varying quantity. In short, as William H. Gilman noted, "He [Dewey] was asserting, of course, what he had believed for years, the primacy of process over product, the fascination with the ways and the effects of thought rather than thought itself."

Sir Alec Clegg and Barbara Megson write in *Children in Distress:* "the object of teaching is not to convey knowledge but to excite a determination in the child to acquire it for himself." But must we choose between process and product? Can we not have both? Why set up this either/ or objective? Why not simply say that the object of teaching is to convey knowledge and to excite a determination in the child to acquire it for himself?

Dr. Eugene E. Dawson, president of Redlands Univer-

sity, said in his inaugural address: "It is not the subject
matter that determines the character of studies as *liberal
studies,* it is, rather, the way in which subject matter, as
a form of discipline, is approached that is decisive." Why
the dichotomy? Clearly there is no product without a
process, nor process without a product. It does matter
what you study for a liberal education *and how* you study
it. Some subject matter is more generative of ideas and
applications than others.

Vincent R. Rogers writes in "English and American
Primary Schools,"

> . . . The English teacher accepts the significance of *process*
> over *product* in the education of the child. There seems
> little doubt that English teachers are greatly concerned
> with *how* a child learns, the kinds of questions he asks,
> and the ways in which he goes about resolving them. Over
> the long haul, English teachers believe these learning
> "strategies" will prove to be infinitely more valuable than
> the subject matter.

It is good to learn how to learn, but what do you learn
after you have learned how to learn?

Some say that facts are not important. But facts are
extraordinarily important when arranged in certain relevant and significant ways. This is like saying that it doesn't
matter what you read, it's *how* you read it, e.g., critically
or perhaps creatively. But we won't read anything critically or creatively unless it means something to us, unless
the subject *matters.* Alfred North Whitehead once said:

> The University imparts information, but it imparts it
> imaginatively. At least, this is the function which it should
> perform for society. . . . This atmosphere of excitement,
> arising from imaginative consideration, transforms knowl-
> edge. A fact is no longer a bare fact: it is invested with
> all its possibilities. It is no longer a burden on the mem-
> ory: it is energizing as the poet of our dreams, and as
> the architect of our purposes.

Whitehead favors the imparting of information but asks that it be transmitted imaginatively so that the fact itself is transformed and is no longer a bare fact.

I wish to repeat that the issue is not process versus product, form versus content, or method versus subject matter. It is rather the kinds of processes used to produce certain products. Surely we would not say it doesn't matter *what* your final product is; what matters is *how* you produced it. If so, we forget that the product pre-exists in the processes, or, as Emerson put it, "The ends pre-exist in the means." The issue really is the kind of product desired. If we expect the immature to produce a mature product, and if in the process we help the child too much and put excessive attention on "correctness," then we have set up a goal or a product that many of us would find unacceptable.

In every subject field taught in school we must come to terms with the concept of process-product. We see this clearly in teaching composition. According to James R. Squire speaking on the topic, "A composition Program for the Future," at the annual conference on the Illinois Association of Teachers of English in October, 1966, "Too much of our attention presently is centered on the products of writing assignments rather than on the processes of writing, and it is the process that we are essentially trying to improve." What does the author mean by process and product? Perhaps he means that at the outset we should not so emphasize the finished product that the child feels his means (processes) are not adequate to reach the desired ends (products).

Sidney Sulkin says in the introduction to *The Challenge of Curricular Change* that "The new curriculum emphasizes the understanding of principles rather than the acquisition of information." Why the "rather than"? You cannot have principles without information nor information without some kind of principles, some kind of structure. Indeed, courses in principles of education, economics, and other fields have sometimes been weak because principles were overemphasized and supporting details underemphasized.

Indeed product and process must not be separated, any more than we would separate form and content. To do so would be like saying to a batter trying to improve his batting average, "It's your form that counts, not whether you hit the ball." However, the purpose of improving the form is to improve the hitting, just as the purpose of the process is progressively to create a product. Perhaps we can partly resolve the dilemma by saying that the process *is* a product. Excellent processes will result in excellent products. So the cycle continues: process—product—process—product—process.

I believe that the way we think about process and product profoundly influences the curriculum of the school. We can think of our world as "in process," or as finished, completed—a product, the end of a series of steps. It is then seen as a fixed world with already available numbers, words, parts of speech, and completed historical events, a world described in textbooks, encyclopedias, films, recordings, and exhibits.

I would reject an either/or proposition and substitute a both/and. There are basic facts to be learned—words, principles, generalizations, and concepts. The issue is not whether there are basic facts and ideas but how they should be learned. For example, I believe that students should learn certain prefixes, suffixes, and roots. But I am strongly opposed to learning them unsystematically by sheer memorization.

Much of what we do in school deals with the ideas the society has already produced. To live the examined life, however, means that we do more than accept past products—we must examine them. Obviously we cannot examine everything at once, but over the long run we can articulate and evaluate the "inarticulate major premises" which Justice Oliver Holmes, Jr. talked and wrote about.

A major issue in all learning deals with the processes by which learning experiences become structured, organized, mapped, patterned, clustered, and systematized. We group experiences, using some kind of framework, paradigm, algorithm, précis, schema, summary, matrix, model, unit, brief, diagram, category, concept, hierarchy, grid, or outline. We use hierarchies, superordination and subordination, major and minor points. All of these terms indicate a linking, a relating of experience on the basis of their differences and likenesses. Process and product, form and content become fused, structured.

The term "structure" is relevant to the discussion of process and product, form and function, or form and content. When something has structure it also has a set of ordered relationships. A structure is a kind of map, a filing system, or a way of classifying relationships. To shift from the old grammar to the new requires a different way of thinking about, or structuring, the English language. Einstein's concept of relativity profoundly shifted the structure of modern physics.

If we structure the world as Communist and anti-Communist, then we are committed to an approach in our relationships with the Communist world which is based on a fallacy—the implication that Communism is the same the world over. A world that is too neatly structured and too simply ordered has little room for creativity or novelty. But an unstructured world or an under-structured world leaves us overwhelmed by novelty and by unclassified, hence indigestible, experiences.

Knowledge can be static or it can be dynamic. Static knowledge is knowledge that does not shift, change, or relate itself to other knowledge. It is, in short, inert. For example, many persons will have a static knowledge of the nature of a noun. They may define it as they did in elementary school: A noun is a name of a thing or an idea. But this concept of a noun is static, not dynamic, and fails to meet the standards of modern scholarship.

A prejudice is static knowledge. It is unexamined, unchanged knowledge which has been uncritically accepted at face value. The essence of dynamic knowledge is the expectation of change and the developing of means to cope with it. The characteristic of dynamic knowledge is knowledge that is constantly being shifted, reclassified, and rethought. It is not on a rigid either/or basis. It can and must be changed.

There is another order of change or process, namely, the changes in the individual himself—from birth to infancy, to childhood, adolescence, middle age, old age, and death. The life processes go on and the needs for new experience change, sometimes gradually, sometimes abruptly.

Some of this change is a catching-up, some of it is an adjusting *to* and adjusting *of* one's activities to swift change. The social catching-up required today is tremendous. Unfortunately some instructors and administrators have "plateaued," settled down mentally, feel no need to adjust, do not want to be disturbed. They like the product—why change it?

I have stated that the paradigm of nature is a cycle of process—product—process—product—process. This cycle continues with or without human intervention. But men have learned that natural processes can be altered by human intervention and that they themselves can be a dynamic part of the change process.

Some say that we should see everything as process. Process, however, is best seen as on a continuum. At one end of the continuum there are slow changes—in rocks, glaciers, the moon, the sun. All are decaying, oxidizing over aeons of time. We often see them as static products, and in an individual's life they seem unchanging. But they are changing, although slowly.

There is value in thinking about these products of nature and of civilization which are our social and individual inheritance. But it is one thing to accept important contributions of the past graciously and thankfully; it is quite another to be satisfied with mere acceptance of a completed product. And since our world and our lives are not finished, we must also see the world as a process. The world we came into was unfinished and we can participate in the never-ending finishing process.

Further, we cannot satisfactorily receive a product which we do not understand, and to understand often means that we ourselves must examine a process carefully and try it out. When information is handed over for un-thinking memorizing we do not make it our own. Indeed, unless we can experiment with it, experience it, process it, we may never *own* it. To receive is to conceive.

Men can therefore choose to intervene and bring their experiences to bear on the situation. There is, however, a real difference between natural and man-made processes. Men can put their varied experiences together in many ways to change natural processes. To do this well, they must be sensitively aware of "choice points," forks in the road, points at which processes can be changed. Men change when they have this awareness of choice and of their responsibility to make these choices.

Irwin Edman put it this way in his Foreword to *Creative Evolution* by Henry Bergson:

> Memory in action is not a dead deposit; it is a living and functional focusing of energies. It is life at the acme of attention, creation, and decision. Memory is life cumulated and brought to bear as alternatives of action, as impell-ingly realized possibilities of choice. Memory is the living reality, the past felt, those moments of heightened con-sciousness which we feel as suggested opportunities to make the future.

The opportunity for choice makes the difference be-tween a closed society and an open society, where creative impulses can reduce regimentation and routine formulas. Fixity and convention can be replaced by flow and spon-taneous freedom, thus opening up the vistas of prophets and poets, seers and saints. If a sense of creative choice is introduced into the flow of process, the process itself is changed, hence the product as well.

The richest experiences of life are perceived at points of choice, at the boundaries of our varied experiences.

Theologian Paul Tillich wrote in the introduction to *Religious Realization* that "The boundary is the best place for acquiring knowledge." It is at the boundary point where the alternatives exist, and if one is not the perennial academician, he must choose one alternative and give up the others. Some act but do not think; others think but do not act.

Thus our lives can be seen as both product and process, depending on our perceptions. If the change is slight, we see it as a product. If the change is visible, we see it as a process. We have a similar dilemma with the terms method and materials of instruction—the how and the what. Emerson wrote in 1823, "Style not matter gives immortality." We need not choose between method and materials or style and matter. We need both.

Method and subject matter are unified, not either/or items. According to Dewey, "Method means that arrangement of subject matter which makes it most effective in use. Never is method something outside of the material." Dewey speaks of using method as "simply an effective treatment *of* material—efficiency meaning such treatment as utilizes the material (puts it to a purpose) with a minimum of waste of time and energy. . . ."

Method, therefore, introduces the question of efficiency. For example, a demonstration teacher was working with a group of inner-city second grade children seated in two rows. She gave each child in the first row a book, one by one. When she started to pass them individually to the second row a second grader said, "Let's use a system for doing this," and simply passed them along. He distributed the material with a "minimum of waste of time and energy." Method affects efficiency and organization.

One of our chief teaching-learning problems is how to organize, structure, and relate experiences so that they are easily available for use in solving problems. When we fail to relate, to meaningfully connect our experiences, they will be forgotten or narrowly applied. Sometimes, too, the experiences from which our clusters and concepts are developed are too narrow, too meager, too parochial, too local.

Sometimes we see too few differences and sometimes we see too many. Our classification may be too broad or too narrow. For example, we tend to see arithmetic, spelling, reading, hygiene, geography, and history as separate, unrelated *products*. Actually they all contain similar experiences classified in different ways. Number belongs not only to arithmetic; it is pervasive. We spell when we write. Reading permeates every field of learning. Most experiences have a place and time location. They relate to the past as well as to the present.

We perceive what we *have* perceived, and we perceive it as we have previously classified it, outlined it, schematized it. For example, if we see a part of a circle, we tend to fill in the entire circle, as is shown by the various studies of perception. Our educational problem, then, is to develop a series of systems, designs, and patterns good enough for preliminary classification but flexible enough to allow for necessary changes in the structure.

If a person felt comfortable about the flexible ways in which he classified material, we might expect that he would be constantly shifting and changing his outlook. However, given an inflexible filing system, given an unwillingness to move outside of our stereotyped images, we become afraid of all experience which we can't readily file, and the process of learning becomes stultified.

All effective instruction results in at least two kinds of learning. One is the actual content learned. The other is the learning of the method used in the learning. (Of course, content may be method, and method, content.) As we learn to read, we read to learn. The process of reading produces a product and the product may change the process. The method and the content interact with each other.

For example, a person can improve his reading in two ways. He may pay special attention to such skills as skimming; noting structural clues such as the outline of a paragraph, a chapter, or a book; and improving his attention by asking questions as he goes along (processes). Or he may improve his reading by mastering the actual words or concepts which appear in the reading (products). There is a *how* and a *what* in all learning. If we emphasize the *how*, we are concerned with the process, the method. If we learn the *what*, we are usually paying attention to the product, the content.

The terms product and process are related directly to the idea of *knowing*. In one sense to know is to have knowledge of (a product). In another sense it means coming-to-know (process). The term *growth* enables us to fuse these two ideas. Growth is a *product*—we can see the seed become a mature plant—but it is also a dynamic, shifting process. The seed is both the product of the past and a part of the process of the future.

Knowledge can therefore be both product and process. What you know enters into relationships with other things and ideas; it does not remain inert. Indeed, if it is inert, it is really not knowledge, since it is irrelevant to our purposes. Knowledge is knowing, not static information. Inquiry is a search for relevant relationships.

I have discussed the problem of process-product and noted some of its meaning when applied to instruction. I have noted the fruitless either/or distinctions between form and content, the what and the how, and form and function. John Dewey and James McLellan have commented: "If we may paraphrase a celebrated saying of Kant's, while form without content is barren, content without form is mushy."

Also relevant are these statements by the artist Ben Shahn in *The Shape of Content:*

Form is formulation—the turning of content into a material entity, rendering a content accessible to others, giving it permanence, willing it to the race. . . . Form in art is as varied as the idea itself.

Form and content have been forcibly divided by a great deal of present-day aesthetic opinion, and each, if one is to believe what he reads, goes its separate way. Content, in this sorry divorce, seems to be looked upon as the culprit.

I have said that form is the shape of content. We might now turn the statement around and say that form could not possibly exist without a content of some kind. It would be and apparently is impossible to conceive of form as apart from content. . . .

Life is a unity. Sometimes we set up an apparent dichotomy, not to choose one or the other, but rather for emphasis, for priority, a way of looking at a situation. Thus, for purposes of study, we may emphasize either product or process, form or content, method or materials. But there is no product without a process, no process without a product. Form and content go hand in hand, as do methods and materials. Life is whole. Therefore, when we write process-product we should see the hyphen not as separating two words but as joining them together.

CHAPTER VIII

A Tailor-Made Curriculum

All planned instruction embodies an image of a certain kind of person as an outcome of the instruction. I shall assume that the chief goal of the school and the college is to develop the thinking, sensitive, mature person. To be such a person is to fully realize one's potential and to discover and develop hidden powers. It means to be governed by thoughtful choice, neither manipulating others nor manipulated by them. Our instructional programs must assume that everybody wants to be a somebody and nobody wants to be a nobody. All persons should be given an opportunity to reach the maturity of selfhood.

A thinking, mature person does his own choosing. He is able to reason and is, therefore, reasonable. To think is to have both concern and responsibility for knowing the critical antecedents of one's actions and their consequences. To think maturely is to move one's self out of a narrow "me-centered" life and into a circle of "we-centered" persons.

A sensitive person adds disciplined emotion to disciplined thinking. To say that he has values is to say that he is a valuing person. To have values is to weigh them and then set priorities, which are considered from the point of view of what they do to persons. A sensitive person is empathetic, is able to put himself into the shoes of other persons, and lets them put on his. When he can take charge of his own life, he has become mature.

To develop the thinking, sensitive, mature person requires a tailor-made curriculum for each person, in short, an individualized and personalized curriculum fitted to the needs and abilities of the learner. Can we tailor a program that builds strongly on individual differences? In so doing, can we also provide for the socializing experiences by which we build a society based on the consensus of the governed?

Glen Heathers of the University of Pittsburgh provides this definition: "Individualized education consists of planning and conducting with *each* [my italics] student, general programs of study and day-to-day lessons that are tailor-made to suit his learning needs and his characteristics as a learner."

Developing The Tailor-Made Curriculum

Considerable discussion centers on how teachers can tailor a curriculum for students, but only limited discussion on how students can tailor a curriculum for themselves. The student and his teacher must work this out together. Some programs of individualized instruction assume a series of highly structured learning tasks, prepared by the teacher or by an outside source, through which all students move at varying rates of speed. The diet is the same, but the spoonfuls vary in size. Time spent is individualized, but the subject matter remains the same. Or, putting it in different terms, all start on page 1 of the textbook, but some reach the last page before others. Obviously, this is a limited and unacceptable concept of individualized instruction.

If instruction is to be tailor-made for the learner, we shall require a revolutionary change in schools and colleges. The needed learning experiences need not always be carried on in the presence of a teacher, nor are they necessarily step-by-step. Learning might take place in large or small classes, in face-to-face tutoring, in groups of two or three, or in independent study. Viewing a children's television program at home could be a planned element in a tailor-made curriculum.

Even though we know better, we act as though all group or individualized instruction requires a formal course or a set of courses. We assume that these courses must be taught by a teacher who is physically present and that his or her personal warmth and wisdom are a necessary factor in helping students to learn. But even now the teacher is not physically present to help the student with his homework, nor are the teacher's instructions for that homework always adequate. One aim of William S. Gray's approach, described in *On Their Own in Reading,* was to produce independence in word-attack skills. Similarly, we want to help all students be on their own in mathematical thinking, in creative writing, in social studies, and in making critical life choices. We want to instruct all individuals so that they can instruct themselves. Unless we work toward this objective we shall produce many graduates who have no further interest in learning and whose talents remain understimulated, and therefore underdeveloped.

Other ways in which programs could be individualized include credit for self-study programs, such as correspondence courses, or for advanced placement examinations. By using these two methods I earned a bachelor's degree at the University of North Dakota in 1921 and spent less than three years on campus. Advanced placement by examination has been widely used and will sharply increase as the concepts of accountability, and program, planning, and budget systems make greater headway.

Another way to individualize instruction with limited curriculum change is to develop programs for independent study. This is being explored, but there are still many complexities involved in its successful operation. Scott D. Thomson, superintendent of the Evanston (Ill.) Township High School, one of the distinguished American high schools, after experimenting with increased independent study (a form of individualized instruction) said that:

> Many students responded well to this concept. . . . A more careful analysis, however, dampens the optimism. It appears that some students do not fare so well. Those who achieved poorly under the traditional system of tight class structure tend to achieve even less well today under the modular schedule. . . . Opportunities for independent study were ignored even when the student selected the area of exploration. . . . It becomes apparent that independent study does not equate with the individualization of instruction. The benefits of individualization do not automatically arise from an open schedule. Rather, they come from a more thoughtful design of instructional strategies. . . .

Obviously, independent study, a key goal of the school or college, needs more careful study and experimentation before launching it as a cure-all. You cannot simply go into it; you must grow into it.

Let us look further into ways in which instruction can be tailored to meet the specific needs of learners. How would you develop a curriculum to teach 3,000 specific words to a group of young children? Would you specify a certain number of words to be learned each week, each month, each year? Would you classify these words according to roots, prefixes, and suffixes, and teach these word parts in an orderly, purposeful way? Would motivation be a difficult problem? If so, what special motivations would you set up, what rewards would you give for excellent performance? Would you give marks and special awards?

Actually, of course, this question is a trap. The typical child starting first grade already knows about 3,000 words. But curiously enough, this learning did not grow out of an orderly, programmed, subject-matter curriculum, nor was it individualized in any formal way. This is not to say it was disorderly or unplanned. Parents tutored and arranged certain experiences, but no one arranged the vocabulary experiences in a logical, planned fashion. The words were learned through social interaction.

Some instruction is and should be carefully and formally arranged; some is not and should not be. Our problem is to know when to use informal, unstructured methods and when to use formal, structured ones. And we also must ask: What are the educational and instructional environments that are best for children who differ significantly from each other?

Students Teach Each Other

In Chapter 1, I mentioned a four-year-old boy who spoke Urdu, Swahili, and English. His parents had not taught him Swahili, because they did not know the language. He had not taken the usual courses in college—Swahili 401, 402, 403. Who taught him? Kushvant's teachers were chiefly his own four- and five-year-old friends in Africa. No one has yet suggested that we invite an "illiterate" four-year-old boy to teach our college courses in Swahili, but it might be worth trying. Indeed, the 3,000 words which the average child knows at the age of six were taught to him by parents and by other children. Might we then individualize instruction by having children teach each other? Each child would try to learn what he was ready to learn or needed to learn.

I watched Kim Lyle, a sixth-grade pupil in Flint, Mich., read "'Twas the Night Before Christmas" to a small group of second-grade children. She stopped from time to time and asked, "What's happening in this picture?" "How many deer are there in this picture?" "Did Santa Claus come down the chimney?" "Do you think this man's name is St. Nick?"

One child asked, "Where's Rudolph?"

Kim displayed a big picture of Santa's toys and asked, "What will the children do with all these toys?"

One reply was, "They'd break 'em up."

Later she stopped and said, "See all that stuff there in the picture? Who do you think put them there? Did Santa put them there?" When she came to the word "rose" used as a verb, Kim inquired, "What does that make you think of?"

The children said, "A flower."

Kim then asked, "Do you know another meaning for 'rose'?" and a child replied, "He rose up."

College students teach each other in informal cram sessions and also in planned programs, clearly a form of individualized instruction. One instance has been described in B. L. Johnson's *Islands of Innovation Expanding* as follows:

At Los Angeles Valley College sophomore students with high achievement in English tutor freshman English students who need assistance. This is done on a voluntary basis, and tutors serve without compensation. Many of them are planning to become teachers, and find that tutoring gives them early teaching experience.

Dr. Catharine Williams of Ohio State University developed a Teen Tutor Program in which seventh-grade boys and girls taught kindergarten children on a one-to-one tutorial basis. It worked well both for the teachers and the taught. Interestingly enough, most studies have shown that the tutor also learns well in this situation. Emerson put it this way: "It is one of the most beautiful compensations of this life that no man can sincerely try to help another without helping himself."

I often ask members of seminars on communication how much we could teach each other directly without using any materials of instruction other than the personal resources of class members. In one class we discovered that we had persons who spoke French and Spanish fluently, an agronomist, two chemists, two speech majors, specialists in instructional television, and one photographer. It might be fruitful to ask members of a class at any level to write down what they could teach each other, using no outside source of materials. In a class of thirty pupils we should try to have thirty-one teachers—the students plus the teacher.

Broadcasting in Continuing Education

New instructional ideas are emerging that provide access to excellence and bring the instructional experience to the learner. For example, in 1971 the British Open University started with an initial group of about 25,000 students, offering them university level courses and providing access to the ablest professors by using radio, television, and printed materials. According to Arthur Marwick, Professor of History at the Open University, they are "pioneering a new technology for teaching to vast numbers" and he notes that they are also "pioneers in a purely academic and scholarly sense."

In *The Listener* (March 12, 1970), Marwick notes six major components of the Open University program:

(1) The academic staff is comparable in quality to conventional universities.

(2) They make use of the highly experienced BBC personnel.

(3) Regional organizations provide tutoring and counseling services.

(4) Educational technologists guide and encourage the academics in the effective presentation of their teaching material.

(5) Media production is a joint responsibility of the academics and educational technologists.

(6) Correspondence services are available from the general post office which sends out and receives material to be sent to tutors.

He also makes the point that the teachers in the Open University "*must very clearly set out just what it is they expect their students to be able to do at the end of a course,* [my italics] which they could not do at the beginning of it." In short, instruction is programmed.

Other movements have a similar aim, namely to provide means by which "more people of all ages can enroll in formal and informal programs of education no matter where they live, their age, or social economic condition." This is a description of the school proposed by the Governor's Commission on Education in Wisconsin in *The Open School:* "Program inputs will be made available to the Open School Teams from all existing state and private educational institutions, from WLA approved libraries, from selected museums, civic centers, from Regional Materials Centers, from all other established agencies on a contractual basis."

Each course will use such methods as ". . . lecture (live, individual tutoring, demonstration, educational games and simulation, programmed workbooks, computer-aided instruction, audio-visual teaching machines, audio tapes, instructional television, work projects, transparencies, motion pictures and single-concept films, direct manipulation laboratories, verbal laboratories, homework exercises, filmstrips, seminars, and reference textbooks."

In 1971 the State University of New York at Albany, with the help of the Carnegie Corporation and the Ford Foundation, inaugurated an "external degree" program which will enable qualified individuals to earn undergraduate degrees by means of independent study. This program was based on experiences gained with the College Proficiency Examination Program. The response to this program has been overwhelming. (Further information can be obtained by writing to the Director, College Proficiency Program, State Education Department, Albany, N. Y. 12224.)

Through its national network, NHK (the Japan Broadcasting Corporation) has presented a wide-ranging program of continuing education. This has included a home-study course leading to a high school diploma and noncredit courses with texts available at newsstands. It is highly significant that in 1971 NHK was planning television programs which would enable an individual to earn a college degree through home study.

Correspondence Study
The development of individualized courses of study is more widespread than many realize. I refer especially to the U.S. Armed Forces Institute (USAFI), Madison, Wis., correspondence courses. Few realize the magnitude of their accomplishments or the high educational level of the enlisted men. Dr. W. L. Brothers, USAFI deputy director for education, reported in 1970 that "almost 80 percent of the Army's enlisted personnel have a high school education as compared with only 30 percent in World War II." Brothers also noted that more than 300,000 U.S. servicemen are tak-

ing courses from USAFI, which offers over 200 courses in six subject areas. More than six million soldiers, sailors, airmen, and marines have enrolled since the beginning of the program in 1942.

Courses are given on the pre-high school, high school, and technical level. Colleges and universities also participate, offering some 6,000 different college credit courses through forty-six schools. Credit acceptances range from twelve hours by the University of Maryland to sixty at the University of Omaha. Most high schools recognize USAFI courses. An estimated two million military personnel have attained high school equivalency credits by passing the battery of general educational tests. Forty-seven percent of USAFI enrollments were in group study classes.

The value of correspondence study as a way to individualize instruction has long been recognized, but the following points need to be considered:

(1) Correspondence puts a heavy responsibility on the learner for independent study.

(2) The effectiveness of the correspondence course will depend upon the quality of the study materials. Many of the procedures used in programmed instruction should be helpful here. The language should be clear and interesting, and not written in professorial jargon.

(3) Instruction need not be entirely by written correspondence. There can be some meetings with the instructor—perhaps as a group activity at the start of a course. Some "correspondence" by telephone is a useful procedure for teacher-student interaction; the personal touch in correspondence study is important.

(4) New types of material—filmstrips, films, television, amplified telephone, computers, film and tape cassettes, recordings, and videotapes—may be used in a systematic way to teach a course.

(5) Improved testing systems for units covered will enable the individual learner to diagnose his progress and apply needed remedial procedures.

(6) The instructor can set up a meaningful dialogue with

the student by means of his written comments. I experienced this in the several undergraduate courses I took by correspondence from the University of North Dakota in the early twenties.

(7) With carefully graded materials of instruction the student is less likely to drop out because of discouragement over some unnecessarily hard lessons.

More than we realize, and this is true both of high school and college, the high school dropouts often drop in again for further instruction. It suggests that our present formal approach to instruction may sometimes be ineffective. In designing educational systems which prepare students for lifelong learning we must, therefore, also include superior, carefully pretested self-instructional materials. Students must learn how to learn and develop a taste for learning. Only then can we realize the magnificent possibilities of a tailor-made instructional program.

Learning Without a Teacher

The amount of self-instruction after graduation from high school or college will increase sharply in the future. What kind of instruction is needed to prepare adults for this type of teaching? In a study entitled "Learning Without A Teacher," Allen M. Tough of the Ontario Institute for Studies in Education comments on his detailed study of a group of forty college graduates who had engaged in some forms of self-instruction. His suggestions often fit the self-instructional needs of elementary and secondary students:

(1) . . . many adults who decide to teach themselves some large and difficult body of knowledge and skills do so quite successfully. . . .

(2) The self-teachers received an astonishing amount of assistance, and they obtained it from an equally astonishing number of individuals. Certainly it is erroneous to think of the self-teacher as a person who plans and manages his self-teaching alone and without human assistance. . . .

(3) . . . students should be trained in self-teaching in order to become *competent* self-teachers. . . .

(4) Practice in learning individually from television, tape recorders, recorders, record players, and programmed materials may widen the scope of methods used by self-teachers. . . .

(5) . . . educators might experiment with various sorts of printed materials and special facilities such as individual motion picture viewers to see whether these, too, can be made especially helpful for the self-teacher. By evaluating the effectiveness of such experimental programs, professional educators will learn how to stimulate, prepare, and assist people who continue learning throughout their adult years.

Flexibility in the Tailor-Made Program

What is called for in all instruction is a more thoughtful, flexible grouping of individuals for instructional purposes— sometimes in a one-to-one relationship, sometimes in an "audience" of 20 to 30 million people. This new flexibility can be achieved by combining old and new tools of communication, many of which do not require face-to-face explanations and which use modern media of instruction. The learner will have ready access to classroom teachers and to mediated teachers.

There will be carefully programmed courses for learners with varied purposes. Individually Prescribed Instruction (IPI) is an example. There are many others, especially for professional or vocational development. Sometimes these programs are correlated with intensive study through short courses, as in business or in the armed forces. We also have the relatively inexpensive amplified telephone conversation or discussion which is still in its infancy. For example, a professor can easily and quickly tap the intellectual resources of a community or of the nation by a phone call. The class does not need to go to the specialist; he comes to them via phone.

The possibility of sharp change in future methods and materials of instruction is heightened by these three factors:

(1) Parents have more education today and can increas-

ingly provide learning centers in the home. These can include all kinds of books and reference sources, tape recorders, self-instructional materials, films, videotape, television, newspapers, and aquariums.

(2) There will be heavier pressure by parents for improved instruction, and they are increasingly aware of ways of organizing to get improved schools.

(3) More parents will be instructing themselves by using modern media.

Breaking the Instruction Lockstep

This call to individualize instruction, to develop a tailor-made curriculum for each child, suggests that previous instruction has *not* been individualized. Obviously many teachers do their best to help each child individually with his problems. But, unfortunately, most children in a typical school use the same textbook, study the same topic at the same time, are examined at the same time, and graduate together four years later from high school or college.

Homework assignments are likely to be similar, although some unplanned individualization of instruction may occur at home. There may also be some differentiation of assignments between classes of less and more able students. The abler students may receive some kind of enrichment work as a "reward" for finishing a unit early. However, giving credit based on a mastery test for a course without regular class attendance is not yet common.

The time has come when we should tailor the curriculum for individual learners. We are making a good beginning, but most children and young people still are subjected to a rigid curriculum. Indeed, as I noted earlier, there is no good reason why this prescribed time schedule needs to be rigidly adhered to. Many students could finish elementary and high school in eleven years and college in three. The professional schools are shortening their curricula and exploring new approaches to instruction. Tailor-made programs of study using increasingly larger amounts of independent learning can play an important part in this change.

The Carnegie Commission on Higher Education reported in 1970 that "We should neither overinvest the time of students nor the resources of society in higher education. . . . The length of time spent in undergraduate college education can be reduced roughly by one-fourth without sacrificing educational quality." Dr. Logan Wilson, president of the American Council on Education, has said: "There is an unreasonable stretchout in formal education. I am heartily in favor of quickening the pace. . . . If you can earn a bachelor's degree in three years why take four? I got my baccalaureate in three years, although I did it by going to summer school."

The emphasis in this chapter has been on developing a tailor-made curriculum for and with the student, part of a long-range program to help all persons become fulfilled. Lucien Price quotes Alfred North Whitehead as saying: "We never seem to have found a way to elicit the complete spread of man's capabilities."

It is true, as Fred T. Tyler and William A. Brownell say in "Individualizing Instruction," NSSE Yearbook (1962), that "individual differences are real, inevitable, ineradicable, desirable, and, indeed essential." However, our methods for systematically capitalizing on individual differences are grossly inadequate. Somehow or other we do not know how to discover and fulfill uniqueness.

Some teachers, for example, are aware of their own uniqueness, but may not treat students as unique and different. We still have the lockstep in education which Frederic L. Burk, president of the San Francisco State Normal School, criticized over sixty years ago. We assume that the graded textbook will usually take care of the differences in ability. Yet the evidence is clear that in all fields of instruction there will be sharp variation of abilities within a specific grade. Typically, in the fifth grade or above there will be six or seven grade levels of variation in reading ability. New methods and materials of instruction are necessary to meet and honor these differences. A tailor-made curriculum for every child coupled with an excellent learning resources center is still some distance in the future. However, as Victor Hugo said in effect, "There is nothing mightier than armies except an idea when its hour has come."

CHAPTER IX

A Life Management Curriculum

People at work or at play are engaged in their major enterprise, managing their own lives. They are managing their time, their energy, their money, their relations with other people, and their communication. Some perform these actions with grace and style, and with few wasted motions. They know what they want to do, and they do it well; they are good managers. They choose wisely and are concerned with the short and long-term consequences of their choices.

Others manage their lives clumsily or even badly. They run out of money before they run out of month and often pay high rates of interest for borrowed money. They are often tired and spiritless, and feel that they are not quite "up to it." Their unorganized, disorganized, and unplanned lives are filled with envy, rancor, petty gossip, and prejudice. "Someone," they feel and say, "has it in for me." They wallow in self-pity and crowd the divorce courts. They do not know how to manage their lives.

We do not have a well-planned life management curriculum in the schools, and this has serious consequences for all students: one-fourth of all high school students drop out before they graduate; another fourth graduate but do not go to college; and one-half attempt some form of higher education and of these about half (or less) finish college. Think of the social waste involved in this evidence of poor social planning.

How can we develop a curriculum which is not distorted by increasing pressures of college entrance standards? How can we help all students get an education which will prepare them for life and also prepare them for college or some form of advanced study? How can we help students meet the challenge of an unpredictable future by learning how to learn and developing a zest for learning? How can we guide students in the critical choices, the big consequential decisions they will make during high school and after?

I propose a Life Management Curriculum. Its ingredients may require new courses, but more often they will emerge as new emphases in old courses.

Awareness of Values

A key ingredient would be a rigorous self-examination of one's own values, by teachers as well as the students. We would concern ourselves with both individual and social values. Students would examine the social values inherent in our great documents—the Declaration of Independence and the Constitution and its Preamble, Articles, and Amendments. Students would study the meaning of law and order, and learn how differently it is perceived by different people. They would see to what extent we in the United States have access to powerful ideas and are provided with a forum for discussing varied beliefs. They would examine critically the abstract term "the public welfare" and figure out what it means in local situations. They would examine the values stated in the Pledge of Allegiance to the flag: What does it mean to have "one nation . . . indivisible, with liberty and justice for all"? How, specifically, do you develop "brotherhood from sea to shining sea"?

The curriculum for building allegiance to democratic ideals would not be a catalogue of items to be memorized.

Rather, it would recognize that within the documents noted and in other sources broadly labeled "the humanities" one may discover and face up to the perennial issues confronting free men. Free men are in charge of their own lives; they make discriminating choices and study the consequences.

We would help students become aware of the key values in their conscious and unconscious choices. They would analyze the traits of men and women whom they admire and wish to imitate. They would discuss their own picture of success, the ingredients of the good life, and the difference between using their education to get ahead *of* other people or ahead *with* them.

Students in search of adult models would inquire about the values of such contemporary leaders as Ralph Nader and John Gardner, of presidents of big businesses, well-known members of Congress, mayors of cities, bankers, doctors, teachers, policemen, carpenters, and truck drivers. Whose interests are they serving? Are they the kind of adults who "put in" more than they "take out"? Can we develop an instructional program which might sharply increase the number of mature, unselfish leaders worth imitating?

Bernice Fitz-Gibbon, advertising and merchandising consultant for *Seventeen* magazine, commented as follows at a fashion clinic for the "back-to-school fashion concept":

> Your fashion department is the wooing chamber. Get the teen-age fly to come into your parlor and little by little the web will be spun. Then when the girl marries, you haven't lost a customer. You've gained a gold mine.

Miss Fitz-Gibbon called the teen-age girl "a woman with means" with "a passion for possession," and urged retailers to go after "the teen tycoons, not in the sweet by-and-by, but in the much sweeter now-and-now. What a bitter epitaph for a world in ruins: They had a passion for possession.

The examination of values in the Life Management Curriculum would help students understand that prejudice blinds all of us a little and some of us a lot, that persons

ordinarily wise in their actions may have blind spots lead-
ing to foolish actions. Mayor LaGuardia of New York
City once acknowledged this tendency, saying ruefully,
"When I make a mistake, it's a beaut!"

We might, for example, ask students in the fourth grade
what they especially liked about Laura Ingalls Wilder's *The
Little House in the Big Woods,* and why the children in this
book enjoy working with their parents on the farm. We
would ask teachers to discuss the values involved in the children's story *Crow Boy* by Taro Yashima, which discloses the
values of those who emphasize the symbolic world but ignore the rich experiences all around them. The book shows
the values of Chibi, a little Japanese boy who communes
with nature.

In literature students might read Sophocles' great work
and discuss Antigone's decision to bury her brother, an en-
emy of the state, and in so doing forfeit her own life. When,
if ever, are we justified in breaking the law, as Huck Finn
did in helping a Negro slave escape? What do you owe the
state, anyway? What are our rights and our responsibilities?
Was Thoreau justified in his refusal to pay taxes which went
to support the Mexican war?

Communication

Another element in a Life Management Curriculum
would be effective communication. It would help students
get in touch and keep in touch with the best ideas in the
world. This would require the mastery of effective study
skills and a higher level of reading. It would require a new
type of learning resource center with easily available media
of communication—films, recordings, filmstrips, computer
terminals, maps, globes, models, television equipment, film
and tape cassettes. It would require an inventory of community resources, human and material, for planned instructional use.

Effective communication would mean more emphasis on
thoughtful discussion; rigorous debate; critical evaluation

of newspapers, magazines, television, and radio; and more learning in small groups. Students would work for depth and concentration in one or more areas and develop taste and skills for continued independent study.

They would practice critical reading, listening, and observing. They would learn how to tell truth from falsehood, fact from opinion, the phony from the real, and the beautiful from the tawdry. They would develop taste and a sense of discrimination in literature, music, and fine arts. They would actively study the nature of evidence and the characteristics of clear and logical thinking. Students would learn that there is no black-and-white answer for everything, that there are often gray areas, and that many statements need qualification. The cartoon, for example, is a powerful persuader but, as newspaper man Adolph Ochs once noted, "It can't say, 'yes, but.'"

The student would not only master the receiving of communications through reading, listening, and observing, but would also master the production skills of writing, speaking, and visualizing. Students now write themes for the teacher of English who checks to see whether they are "correctly" written. Further, we do not adequately prepare students to become skilled in the art of discussion. Nor have we shown much concern with developing persons who can visualize by drawing, painting, photographing, or sculpturing. The camera is ever present outside the school, but photography is not commonly included in the school or college curriculum.

The mass media would get our special attention in a Life Management Curriculum. Curiously, the media to which we are exposed most often—the newspaper and magazine, the radio, the television, and records—get scant attention in the school. If the aim of the school is to help students make better life choices, then increased attention must be given to the thoughtful use of mass media. The teachers of English and social studies need to bear down much harder in this area.

Emotional Soundness

Our Life Management Curriculum would help young-sters learn how to work closer to the upper limit of their emotional, mental, and physical powers, to test the limits of their endurance. Many people, young and old, have not tapped their inner resources; they go through life with their brakes on, suffering from remediable emotional handicaps. The booklet *Emotion and Physical Health,* published by the Metropolitan Life Insurance Company, says:

. . . almost 50 percent of all people seeking medical attention today are suffering from ailments brought about or made worse by such emotional factors as prolonged worry, anxiety, or fear. Emotional tensions often play a prominent role in certain kinds of heart and circulatory disorders, especially high blood pressure; digestive ailments, such as peptic ulcer and colitis; headache and joint and muscular pains, skin disorders; and some allergies.

How could the necessary experiences for an improved program in health education (both mental and physical) be ensured? Teachers would have to become more sensitive to the causes of their own emotional aches and pains and those of children and young people. All teachers would help students safeguard their physical health and raise issues about the physical and mental health of our nation. We all know of the anxieties of children and young people regarding their grades and their preparation for college entrance requirements. Some of these anxieties arise from the nature of the present curriculum, but they also arise from influences in the environment.

This is only a part, however, of the problem of emotional health. Students need to become aware of the many unrelenting pressures to get them to consume, to buy on impulse, and to open a charge account. We would expect them to study advertising and to become sensitive to the values appealed to. What appeals, for example, are made to get students to smoke cigarettes, to consume liquor, or to use or avoid drugs?

A Life Management Curriculum would develop a general

motivation to learn. We would accept the principle that success is the best motivator. Temporary failures in an atmosphere of success are inevitable, and do no lasting harm, but a daily diet of failure is a discouraging and debilitating experience. Certainly we can provide a range of experiences wide enough to allow everyone to achieve success in learning. We know that students schooled in failure reject themselves, feel worthless, drop out of school, and become cynical, belligerent, or indifferent.

Sometimes these failures lie in personal relationships with others. We must, therefore, help students learn how to enter imaginatively into the lives of others and to have the courage to let others enter into theirs. Literature taught imaginatively and with insight will help students understand a Huck Finn, a Billy Budd, and a Malcolm X, and provide the depth in communication that can be found in great literature.

High school students can learn that they are not the first to suffer the humiliation of rejection or the feeling of great joy in simple pleasures. You cannot have success without some failure, but we can learn to profit from our mistakes. Further, a good school provides guidance at those key points which may lead to error or mistaken impressions, with consequent discouragement.

Time and Money

Time is a most precious commodity. How could a Life Management Curriculum help students invest their lifetime to the best advantage, live efficiently and effectively without undue worry and anxiety? They might learn that all of us practice self-deception regarding our use of time. We say that if we had time, we would read the good books, write the letters of appreciation, learn a foreign language, improve our vocabulary, and do more civic work. Actually we find time to do most of the things we really want to do. No man is ever so busy that he cannot take time out to tell how terribly busy he is. But time is finite, and we must choose our priorities on the basis of examined values.

We would help students respect time by seeing that it can be invested with rich returns or squandered carelessly with meager and sometimes dangerous results. The person in charge of his life will learn how to budget time for the things he really wants to do, not throw it away uselessly.

Does the typical school set an excellent example in helping students manage their own time? Yes and no. Philip W. Jackson says in *Life in Classrooms:*

> Indeed, when we begin to examine the details of classroom life carefully, it is surprising to see how much of the students' time is spent in waiting. . . . No one knows for certain how much of the average student's time is spent in neutral, as it were, but for many students in many classrooms it must be a memorable portion.

Differences among students in rates of learning are enormous. Some children finish their work quickly and then wait, patiently or impatiently, for the others to finish. The ablest students may read an assignment four or five times as fast as the least able students. We do not make adequate use of this difference in learning rate.

We waste student time because they are not learning for use but are learning *about*. The ease with which some people can learn *about* by sheer memorizing leads to false notions about the nature of learning. I use learning as meaning incorporation, internalizing, systematizing, and habituating. Half-learning, three-quarters learning, or 90 percent learning is not enough; learning for mastery is needed. Eventually the skill, attitude, or information must be learned to the point of fluency in actual behavior. It must become deeply rooted in one's habit system. For example, in learning to ride a bicycle you can only get an A or flunk. True, abilities to ride a bicycle may vary, but you either can ride a bicycle or you cannot. Almost learning something is not good enough.

All of us possess a large reservoir of latent behavior—the "almost learned". And if this almost learned material, this twilight zone material, is not moved into actual use, it will remain dormant, inert, and perhaps forgotten. One of our biggest sources of learning, then, lies in mastering what we have almost learned. Hundreds of thousands of students have almost learned to develop sensitive human relations, have almost learned to write clear, competent English, or have almost learned to study effectively. But they have reached a plateau after traveling 80-90 percent of the route to mastery, and they need help in traveling the rest of the distance.

The management of money is closely related to the management of time and energy. Think of the importance of key decisions regarding buying an automobile, buying or renting a home, the kind and amount of insurance to buy, the management of one's own business, problems of business law, and methods of record keeping. The decisions we make in spending money have lifetime significance, yet high schools and colleges give meager instruction in this field. The rise of the ombudsman is one sign of heightened interest in the consumer field.

A national survey showed that 44 percent of the people questioned did not know the interest rate on money they had borrowed. Many do not understand the process of compound interest, or know whether there is a financial penalty for paying their mortgage loan ahead of time. They do not realize that on certain charge accounts they may be paying 18 percent interest.

We could meet this problem by introducing modules or units of instruction on everyday economics. Our scheduling processes are becoming more flexible, and it would be relatively easy to introduce units on How to Buy a Car; Buying on the Installment Plan; Investing, Speculating, and Gambling; What is Insurance? I developed such a course in the Skokie Junior High School in Winnetka, Ill., in 1925. The central theme hinged on the key question: What does everybody need to know about investing, insurance, borrowing money, savings and checking accounts, and so on? Individual and governmental concern with consumer education makes it likely that in this decade there will be a marked increase in the materials of instruction available in this field.

Since about half of all students will not enter college, a Life Management Curriculum must give them at least minimum skills for employment. Good attitudes, effective and responsible work habits, thoughtful employer-employee relations, responsive human relationships, and effective communication skills are important in such employment, and will also provide the flexibility needed in a changing industrial world.

Human Values

A Life Management Curriculum must provide continuing practice in the art of humane relationships. The art is not an easy one to practice. Indeed, many people violate their own ideals by unkind, thoughtless behavior, sometimes wrecking their own careers by their insensitivity. They are bold and unfeeling when they should be unassuming and sensitive, and they are apathetic and fearful when they should be involved and courageous.

Every person must learn to control his fears, lest he be controlled by them. It is not strange that Phobos, meaning fear, was the son of the war god Mars. The fearful person communicates his fear to others. Clearly, there is a difference between being aware of danger and fearing it excessively. Mark Twain once said: "Courage is resistance to fear, mastery of fear—not absence of fear."

Justice diminishes fear; injustice creates and nourishes it. The good society replaces fear with courage. Dag Hammarskjold noted that "Life only demands from you the strength you possess. Only one feat is possible—not to run away." And when you run away, even the cowards will pursue you. Rosa Parks, a Negro working woman, did not run away when asked to go to the rear of a bus in Montgomery, Ala. She refused to do so, and her courage has provided a model for young people and for fearful older people the world over. How many white people know and honor her name?

A Life Management Curriculum must provide both living and historical models of people who have related themselves warmly and humanely to those around them. William James, the psychologist and philosopher, once said that the aim of philosophy was to help the student know a good man when he saw one. Further, a humane society honors all its members, not just a chosen few, some of whom may have mastered the arts of publicity. In a Life Management Curriculum we help each other discover our potential, learn what we can do well.

I repeat that everyone wants to be a somebody; no one wants to be a nobody. Many children, young people, and adults have lost faith in their power to be a somebody. They need mentors and guides to lend a helping hand over the rough spots. They certainly do not need punishment for their weaknesses, for they have suffered enough already. They need help in building faith in their own ability to manage their own lives.

A good society is sensitive and gentle, not harsh and rough. It is not rigid; it is flexible, pliant, generous, and courteous. Everyone—young or old, rich or poor, educated or illiterate—can master these qualities. And the opportunity to learn how to behave humanely is the social heritage of every person. Too often we honor "big" names but have not learned to pay our respects to the "little" names. The *Book of Ecclesiasticus* put it this way: "And some there were which have no memorial; who perished, as though they had never been . . . but these were merciful men, whose righteousness hath not been forgotten. . . . Their glory shall not be blotted out . . . but their name liveth forevermore."

If we are to behave humanely toward each other, we must learn how to carry our share of the burdens of society and how to participate joyfully in working with others. We cannot manage our lives well if we have not experienced the discipline of planning and the carrying out of these plans. Thomas Carlyle, the British essayist and historian, once said that we should do the duty which lies nearest us which we know to be a duty. By so doing, the second duty will already have become clear. Nor should we assume that little duties are unimportant.

William Blake, the English poet, noted "He who would do good to others must do it in minute particulars." I have listened to hundreds of students praising some of their professors and teachers. I have been struck by how many of these comments dealt with particulars. A distinguished professor said of one of his professors in graduate school: "On the day I enrolled in graduate school, he noticed that I was just wandering around and took me across the street to have a cup of coffee." A junior high school student who had become a president of a major company told me after a lapse of forty years: "I remember you well. You tried to teach me some Norwegian."

In a Life Management Curriculum relating to better human relations we need to discuss the arts of friendship. "A man, Sir," said Samuel Johnson, "should keep his friendship in a constant repair." In a world filled with pseudosophistication, with much that is phony, this concern with the development of friendship may seem like sticky sentimentality, hardly a competitor with mathematics, or science, or foreign languages for a place in the curriculum. But sensitivity to human values should always rate high on the priorities for the school curriculum.

These comments about a Life Management Curriculum are obviously suggestive, not definitive. They call attention to the fact that the critical choices of individuals are not primarily related to mathematics, linguistics, science, or history. Rather, they are choices of values; of the use of time, energy, and money; of friends or of a mate; and in receiving and expressing ideas. They are the choices on which one must focus the wisdom gained in and outside school.

We are often advised to "think big." Certainly it makes good sense to manage our lives so that we avoid the narrow and provincial, and try to become world citizens. But there is also merit in the advice to "think small." Psychologist and philosopher William James put it this way:

I am done with great things and big things, great institutions and big success, and I am for those tiny invisible molecular moral forces that work from individual to individual creeping through the crannies of the world like so many rootlets, or like the capillary oozing of water, yet which, if you give them time, will rend the hardest monuments of man's pride.

CHAPTER X

On Living Humanely

There are two views concerning the desired atmosphere of a school or classroom. One is that it should be quiet and orderly—"no whispering, please." Children should not be walking around or going to the restroom too often. Smiles, yes; rollicking laughter, no. The display of rich, deep emotion is indecorous. We reward the "good mind."

Another view is that the classroom should be like a good home, including the orderly disorder that comes from doing. Laughter comes easily. Children work together in small groups, moving around when they get tired of what they are doing—stretching their legs, resting their minds, or shifting to another activity. It is not unseemly to display warm, friendly emotion; indeed, it is encouraged. Both the good mind and the good heart are rewarded.

There is danger in seeing teachers and students chiefly as receptacles for receiving and temporarily remembering facts, but not as living, breathing persons with compassionate hearts. The intellectually oriented instructor teaches what he *knows* (and this may be a lot), but he may fail to teach what he *is*. Virgil said, "Many of these things I saw, and some of them I was." Students want to know what their teacher saw, but they also desire the kind of communion

that comes from knowing what he was and is. They want the
teacher's humanity to shine through; they want to see him
or her as a human being who feels joy and pain just as they
do.

A four-year-old girl said to her father, "Daddy, please
laugh." Her father then "laughed" with a "Ho, Ho, Ho!"
She said, "No, not like that, Daddy. Laugh like you used to."
In other words, laugh like you used to before you became so
preoccupied with your work, before you squeezed joy and
laughter out of your life. The adolescent son of a big business executive had no opportunity to talk over a personal
problem with his father. He seriously considered calling his
father's secretary for an appointment, an idea vetoed by his
startled mother.

But we are increasingly concerned with emotions. Daniel
Prescott argues persuasively in *Emotion and the Educative
Process* that the intellectual development of students is not
enough, that it requires the momentum of emotion to make
an experience a rich one. He asks these questions:

> What can be said of the life of the child at school?
> Is it rich in feeling? Has it the tang of exciting dis-
> covery, the testing of the stuff that personality is made of,
> the thrill of feeling that here one *swirls in the stream of
> real life?* [Italics mine.] . . . is there an opportunity to
> enrich life from beginning to end by guiding children
> into and through high moments of vivid, exciting ex-
> perience?

We have always had programs in the humanities in our
colleges, and we increasingly include them in the high
school curriculum. The usual aim of these courses, however,
has not been to produce warm, humane people. For example,
the role of drama as a humanizing element in the university
curriculum has always been neglected. Some professors of
humanities have been imitating the behavioral scientists by
engaging in "scholarly" activities, for example, checking
the various editions of an author's works by computer to
note shifts and changes. But we cannot educate the whole
man unless we use drama and other "touching" experiences.

Tennessee Williams put it this way in "Concerning the Time-less World of a Play," *New York Times* (Jan. 14, 1951):

> Our hearts are wrung by recognition and pity, so that
> the dusky shell of the auditorium where we are gathered
> anonymously together is flooded with an almost liquid
> warmth of unchecked human sympathies, relieved of self-consciousness, allowed to function. . . . Men pity and love
> each other more deeply than they permit themselves to
> know.

Once I asked a high school teacher of literature what his aim was in teaching *The Adventures of Huckleberry Finn*. Was it perhaps to clarify the moral dilemma when the law conflicted with one's moral outlook? On the contrary. His aim, he said, was to show that when Huck was on land, he was in trouble; when he was on water, he had no difficulties. If we cannot develop the emotionally sensitive learner, of what worth is it merely to increase his information?

If we critically read *Huckleberry Finn*, we see that it is more than an adventure story, more than a pleasant escape into a world where you "laze around" most of the day. Twain enables us to live imaginatively in the lives of Huck and Old Jim, portraying a story of love and affection as up-to-date as *To Kill A Mockingbird*.

Twain's Old Jim is a seeker of freedom, a loving father, and a trusted friend. As a father, he is sad when he remembers how he slapped his four-year-old daughter when she did not do what he asked—only to find out a few minutes later that scarlet fever had made her deaf. He is glad when Huck is safe but is ashamed of Huck's trick to fool him into thinking that he dreamed that Huck was gone. Huck says, "I didn't do him no more mean tricks, and I wouldn't done that one if I'd a knowed it would make him feel that way."

The teacher of a literature class in an Ohio high school had read *Flowers for Algernon*, written by Professor Charles Webb of Ohio University in Athens. She was moved and delighted by the story and began thinking about a unit which would combine reading this story with the viewing of the film "Charley," which is based on the book.

Webb was invited to visit the class and accepted. He told them the circumstances leading to his writing of the book, that he had been deeply moved by the question of a retarded boy who had asked him: "Mr. Webb, if I do all the things that you tell me to do, will I be a changed boy?" The high school students were deeply touched by these experiences. Some of the older boys admitted that they had actually cried when they read *Flowers for Algernon*.

We are prone to see humaneness as a single act of a single individual. In a modern urban society, however, this approach is not adequate. Instead, we must treat the problem in depth and trace the intricate web of personal relationships that makes us humane and inhumane. Being humane is both a social and an individual act.

We are not yet ecologically minded, either in human or nonhuman terms. That is, we are insufficiently aware of the relationships that living things have to each other and to their environment. We do not really understand the ecology of humanism as explained in *World Book Encylopedia:* "No living thing—plant or animal—lives alone. Every living thing depends in some way upon certain living and non-living things . . . man's survival and well-being depend on relationships that exist on a world-wide basis." John Donne said it well 300 years ago: "No man is an island . . . any man's death diminishes me, because I am involved in mankind."

We must, therefore, search out and correct those faulty relationships which permit and promote wars and massacres of innocent men, women, and children. What was there in the German culture that permitted, indeed encouraged, the murder of six million Jews? Why did some Americans massacre men, women, and little children in Vietnam? Why did some North Vietnamese do the same thing?

Do you remember the flurry of criticism against the mass media when the first pictures of the My Lai massacres in Vietnam came out? They did not fit our assumptions or conceptions about war. We thought war could be aseptic, that we could burn anonymous people with napalm, and have nice clean killing from the air as at Hiroshima. But it turns out that all war is bloody and cruel; it includes shooting a little boy clinging to his mother and the senseless murdering of civilians. When television reports bad news which discloses our cruelty and brutality, we discount the message and abuse the messenger.

In trying to develop humane relationships we must remember both our successes and our sorrowful failures in being humane. Why does hate come so easily? Why is revenge so sweet? A class might well discuss such questions as they deal with the news of the day and note "man's inhumanity to man." Paul A. Varg, dean of College of Arts and Letters at Michigan State University, points out with penetrating insight in "The Proposed Foundation for the Humanities," *Journal of Higher Education* (May, 1965):

> The values of humanistic pursuits lie in what they do to give the individual a deeper, broader, and richer understanding of himself and his relations to other men, and not alone of his own time and place. The humanist, thanks to his understanding of history, sees the political, economic, and social crises of his generation in the perspective of the past. . . . The humanist knows the endless complexities of individual and social behavior. . . .
>
> Above all, the humanist seeks to understand himself; he sees clearly his capacity for generous feelings, his potential strength of character, no less than the limitations imposed on him by an ego which compels him to view himself as the center of existence.
>
> The study of literature and of the arts provides the means of transcending the limited horizons of individual experience and enables us to view, almost as if they were our own, the experiences of other individuals, other social groups, and peoples in cultures far removed from our own.

Dr. Edward G. Olsen, professor of education at California State College in Hayward, says in *The Community School and its Administration* (April, 1970) that we should challenge youth and adults "to help everybody, all ages, become deeply aware of the vast gulf between our daily democratic declarations and our daily discriminatory dealings. Challenge to help them face frankly and creatively the great human relations problems of our time: war, poverty, racism, overpopulation, environmental pollution, consumer cheating, and all the rest. Challenge, in short, to share ethically in the building of a truly humane society of dignity and decency for all. . . ." Few white people are able and willing to face the fact of their own prejudices in race relations.

The humane person is a responsible person. It is undignified and dehumanizing, therefore, to permit young people to grow up with only light burdens of individual and social responsibility or to permit them to work at undemanding, unchallenging routine tasks far below their potential. It is an affront to the young when we do not show them how to share their strengths with each other. If a twelve-year-old can do a man's job driving a tractor on his father's farm, or a fourteen-year-old use a chain saw, a sixteen-year-old or a twenty-two-year-old city youth can take up some of the heavy burdens of society. Is there any evidence that they have refused to take responsibility for which they are directly prepared?

Those who talk about the irresponsibility of youth must face the fact that many of them are already shouldering a heavy responsibility for building peace, for reducing racial prejudice, and for putting pressures on universities to see that scientists do not permit their professional existence to depend on research in the science of killing. These actions of youth are the actions of humane people.

Further, what appears to be youthful irresponsibility is often a sequel to a responsibility too long deferred. After all, a daily diet in high school and college of memorized answers to fact questions hardly leads to serious, responsible behavior or to a concern for genuine scholarship. Work-study activities are a good start toward developing responsibility, and future instruction will have a heavy infusion of responsible employment. As yet, however, such programs cover only a fraction of high school or college students.

To become richly human, everyone must have a keen

sense of his own potential. Potential comes from the Latin *potens,* meaning powerful. But many people underestimate their latent power and confuse undeveloped power with weakness.

Heavy burdens develop people's powers. We have often thought of Presidents of the United States as being heavily overburdened and overwhelmed by work. It is likely that they are, but they develop the power to meet their responsibilities. Similarly, all of us have latent power for developing our own humanity.

If you ask teachers and others to estimate the percentage of their power that they are using, few say as high as 70 percent and the answer is usually much lower. Fifty percent is a typical figure, but scientists say that many people use less than 25 percent of their potential. This is not because people do not want to do more, or feel that they have already reached the peak of their powers. Rather, it is because the opportunities for power development are not made available. There must be carefully planned experiences through which aspiration can become achievement.

Language can make man human and humane. We learn to know our feelings and desires by crystallizing them into words. There is rich meaning for many of us in such words as communication, self-renewal, creativity, imagination, understanding, compassion, sharing, empathy, comradeship, and appreciation. Sometimes an imaginative artist working with words, images, sounds, paint, stone, or space helps us crystallize our foggy ideas and feelings. Shakespeare put it this way in *A Midsummer Night's Dream:*

> And as imagination bodies forth
> The forms of things unknown, the poet's pen
> Turns them to shapes and gives to airy nothing
> A local habitation and a name.

I have asked many high school and college students what Shakespeare meant when he wrote "He jests at scars who never felt a wound." Some do not understand it, and perhaps it is hard for almost anyone to get the full import of this statement. Yet this statement, which preceded the creation of the word "empathy" by about 300 years, is at the heart of all humane education. Do students and teachers love and pity each other more deeply than they permit themselves to know, as noted in the comment by Tennessee Williams earlier in this chapter? Methods and materials of instruction should enable students to discover the depth of meaning in his penetrating and poignant statement.

How can we help students communicate in depth and learn how to put themselves into the shoes of the other fellow? We have lots of "walking wounded" who do not get a chance to tell where it hurts and to get help in easing the pain. Adolescents and young people hurt when they think of the future; many wonder whether there will be any future at all.

Giving and receiving is a two-way street, and the humane person has learned to do both. A sensitive giver deserves a sensitive receiver. We are all aware of stingy givers, but are we equally aware of stingy receivers who lack the sensitivity, the humaneness, to receive the gift in the spirit in which it was given? The Lord loves a cheerful giver but is disappointed with a churlish receiver.

The root meaning of "gratitude" comes from the Latin *gratus*, which means "pleasing" or "thankful." It is closely related to the words "grace" and "gracious." Gilbert Chesterton, the English author and critic, said that he organized his life around the idea that we should take things with gratitude, not take them for granted.

Many today take for granted their right to criticize their government, their schools and colleges, and their churches. They do have this right, but with it goes an obligation to be aware of the great discipline which was required to develop and improve these institutions. This troubled world has little need for sophisticated irresponsibility. Reduced opportunities for rigorous self-discipline will ruin a society.

If we expect humane treatment from others, it must come because we treat them humanely. And conversely, if we treat them badly, we can expect to be paid back, now or later, in the same coin; love and hate draw compound interest. It has been observed that today the slum is taking its revenge.

Few people realize the difficulties which most Negroes and other disadvantaged minorities have undergone in order to become a professional—a doctor, a lawyer, or teacher—or to finish graduate school. The number of black students whose parents are college graduates or professional people is still very small, although it is increasing sharply. Every Negro who grew up in an atmosphere of poverty and prejudice bears spiritual scar tissue. It is tough for anybody, whether black or white, to be rejected because he cannot meet the requirements of school or college. But to be black, poor, and an inadequate student puts your future in triple jeopardy.

Becoming humane requires a lifetime of self-discipline. The disciplined person knows what he wants to do, knows how to do it, and does it. For example, do we know *what* to do about drugs and drug addiction, and *how* to do it? Are we doing it? *Time* magazine (Dec. 26, 1969) reported that Walter Vandermere had just died from a dose of heroin. Walter was twelve years old and "he learned about hustling, dope, and sex before he was ten. Often he subsisted on potato chips, baloney, and sodas. . . . It was not just heroin that killed Walter . . . he died of his whole life." What disciplines could we impose on ourselves to make the death of this child and hundreds like him increasingly impossible?

Do we know how to build decent houses for everybody? We do. Are we doing it? We are not. Why not? As a nation we lack the disciplined will that makes it possible. We permit dehumanizing housing to exist. In a humane world we try to see that every family has a good home. This is one of the tasks a school or college can help perform.

To build a humane world we must look at the factors which cause dehumanization. Here are some examples:

(1) We dehumanize persons by ignoring them. Eric Fromm, writing in *May Man Prevail*, says: "This new kind of inhumanity . . . is not cruelty or destructiveness. It is more inhuman than that, although perhaps more innocent, if this

were the word. It is the attitude of complete indifference and lack of concern; it is the attitude . . . that administers men as if they were things." Do we ever administer a school or college as if the students were things? How do we manipulate them—overtly and covertly?

(2) We dehumanize and humilate people by not permitting them to become an integral part of the society, by keeping them apart from it. We think they are too young, too old, too black, too rich, or too poor. They become alienated spectators, not participants. They are no longer *engagé*, in Jean-Paul Sartre's term. It is one thing to be temporarily self-detached from a society; it is quite another to become permanently alienated from it.

(3) Some mistakenly assume that the machine is dehumanizing us. Does anyone really believe that he is dehumanized by his electric typewriter or his automobile? Were we dehumanized by the ship, compass, railroad, telegraph, camera, airplane, or television? Hardly. The machine is not the source of dehumanization. Indeed, it may have actually increased our autonomy. These devices are all extensions of man, which can be used for good or bad purposes.

It is good that people dream dreams about a humane society and see visions of a new world. But dreams of utopia can also act as a narcotic. We enjoy the dream but fail to act. We forget that to make our dreams come true we need engineers who take on the tough job of translating dreams into practice. Technology is a means—man determines the end.

What curriculum approach do we use if we are convinced that there is a need for guidance and instruction in how to develop humane values? Can we humanize present studies or introduce new programs, or develop some combination of the two? John Dewey commented in *Democracy and Education* that "Any study so pursued that it increases concern for the values of life, any study producing greater sensitiveness to social well-being and greater ability to promote that well-being is humane study."

We ask these questions then about any program or experience aimed to humanize:

(1) How does this program increase concern for the values of life—help the learner to learn what is worthy of respect and worth promoting?

(2) How will this study produce greater sensitivity to the well-being of every individual and create greater ability to promote well-being?

Every day we are choosing our humane values—whether always to conform or also to be inventive and creative, whether to be open to new experience or closed to it, whether we shall be trained or educated, whether we want to live for the short run alone or both the short run and the long run. We are choosing to love, to be different, or to hate; to perform in the arena of life or to be a cynic on the sidelines.

Failure to develop man's humanity to its fullest will have one of two results. It will make us either apathetic or rebellious. Today we are learning (and learning the hard way) that, as Dickens wrote in *Hard Times*, "all closely imprisoned forces rend and destroy."

In 1959 Stephen Corey, then dean of Teachers College, Columbia University, wrote in *The Child's World: His Social Perception* by Frank J. and Elizabeth W. Estvan:

> Our world will end, it if does, in catastrophe not because today's boys and girls and tomorrow's citizens perceive unrealistically the physical world—be it the universe or the inside of an atom. Catastrophe will come because these children growing up in the midst of the tragic biases of us adults have had insufficient opportunity to perceive realistically the strivings and interrelationships of their fellow men.

Everybody needs uncluttered physical space for himself and his family. But everybody also needs uncluttered mental and spiritual space, the opportunity to think his own thoughts and ideas, to be creative, and to live a rich life. In a humane world there will be a good home for everybody.

INDEX